SAMUEL PETTY LEATHER

GAS ENGINEER OF BURNLEY

1821 to 1889

A David Leather

THE LEATHER FAMILY HISTORY SOCIETY
1993

to the memory of Arnold John Leather

Subscribers to this edition

Deborah M Balijon
Joan E Duncan
Michael J Gibbins
Janet E Grant
Martin and Sunniva Green
Michael Conyngham Greene
Krijn S de Groot
Alan Joseph Leather
Mrs Brenda P Leather
G M Leather

John B and Alison Leather
Margaret Leather
Peter M Leather
Simon R Leather
J Kenneth S Petty
Anthony Petyt
Brian Petyt
Christine and John Rose
Gillian Elliott Smith
Wharfedale Family History Gp

Thanks to British Gas North Western for their kind support.

First published in 1993 by the Leather Family History Society, Woodlands, Panorama Drive, Ilkley, West Yorkshire, LS29 9RA England

© A David Leather 1993

ISBN Paper
0 9520545 0 7

Printed and bound by
J W LAMBERT & SONS
Station Road, Settle, North Yorkshire, BD24 9AA

CONTENTS

	Page
Preface	
1. Early Days	1
2. Formative Years	10
3. Marriage	21
4. The Family In Burnley	35
5. Finale	64
Family trees and maps	71

PREFACE

This short family history, written around the life of my great grandfather, Samuel Petty Leather, has grown out of the wealth of material which has come to light following the recent deaths of my father, Arnold John Leather, and also his sisters Margaret and Hannah Leather.

The material is in the form of letters, notebooks, certificates, newspaper cuttings, photographs and scraps of paper and it is perhaps unusual that such a large amount of useful memorabilia, some of it dating back over 150 years, should have been preserved and passed on from one generation to the next. Added to this are the results of recent research carried out in reference libraries, record and register offices. When arranged in chronological order, copied and catalogued, these items provide a natural story of the life of Samuel Petty Leather.

In the last five years a great deal of new information has been accumulated about the Leather family and, in 1991, Simon R Leather founded the Leather Family History Society.

A D Leather
Ilkley, December 1992

1 EARLY DAYS

One of a large Yorkshire family, Samuel Petty Leather lived roughly in the middle of the nineteenth century which made him a true Victorian. His descendants refer to him affectionately as 'Samuel P' as he always signed his name or used a rubber stamp *Samuel P. Leather*. He also presumably wished to distinguish himself from his first cousin, Samuel Leather who was a year younger, and who became a wool manufacturer in Bradford.

Samuel P had his fair share of misfortune and his early years were a continuous struggle. He had to endure the deaths of three close relatives at critical periods in his life, the first of which was that of his mother at the age of four, a major tragedy which must have influenced his development and outlook considerably. Later, he lost his young first wife, and was to see his eldest son go when still a teenager.

In spite of all his difficulties Samuel P had great determination and ambition to learn all he could, to get on in life and to prosper. As he grew up he had to rely on relatives, particularly his grandfather on his mother's side, after whom he was named, and who gave him help and encouragement at an early stage. From his father he learned surveying and his uncle George Leather gave him his first job at Leeds Waterworks. After three posts in the water industry, spanning twelve years, he moved to the gas industry where he became Manager of Hyde gasworks in Cheshire. Finally, he became chief engineer and manager of

Burnley gasworks, a position he kept for twenty-five years until his death in 1889. He married twice and had two sons from his second marriage, the second son survived to follow him as the next manager of the Burnley gasworks. During his lifetime, Samuel P lived in four major cities, three towns and two villages, all in the north of England.

SAMUEL P'S PARENTS   His father was John Leather, the youngest son of George and Hannah Leather of Wakefield where John was born in 1796. Baptised in Wakefield Cathedral, John later came with the family to live in the village of Beeston, now part of the city of Leeds. John's father, George senior, was chief colliery engineer for William Fenton, a Yorkshire 'coal king' and was responsible for laying out New Park Colliery in Beeston. John's older brothers James and George were both civil engineers. John himself became a land surveyor and architect, married Mary Ann Petty and moved to Sheffield for his business. Later he established himself as an architect in Liverpool where, with his second wife, he lived for 35 years.

Mary Ann Petty was Samuel P's mother, the sixth child of Samuel and Ann Petty. Her father was a baker and flour dealer who in 1817 held the public office of 'Surveyor of Highways for Beeston'. Later, her father had a part interest in Hunslet Hall Pottery which made earthenware. In the 1820's the Pettys had a retail outlet on Briggate, a street in central Leeds, for the sale of china and glass. Mary Ann was born in Beeston in January 1799 and was three years younger than her husband John. She was twenty-one years old on her wedding day.

The marriage of John Leather and Mary Ann Petty took place on the 15th May 1820 in the Parish Church of Saint Peter, Leeds and is recorded in the local parish register which reads as follows:

Marriages solemnised in the Parish Church of Leeds in the County of York.

John Leather of this Parish, Gentleman and Mary Ann Petty of this Parish, Spinster, were married in this Church by Licence (Vicar surr.) this fifteenth Day of May in the Year One thousand eight hundred and twenty by me C. Clapham, Curate.

The marriage was solemnised between us
{ John Leather
{ Mary Ann Petty
In the presence of: Saml Petty.   Low. Eyres.

The certificate is signed by both parties in the marriage and one of the witnesses is Samuel Petty, father of Mary Ann. The other signature is that of the Rev Lawrence Eyres who ran a school in Beeston, known as the Rev L Eyres Academy. Here, two years previously, Mary Ann's sister Eliza learned handwriting at the age of fourteen.

The fact that the couple were married by licence rather than by banns suggests that the families were well off and could not only afford the cost of the licence but preferred the more private affair of a wedding by licence. Soon after their marriage John and Mary Ann moved to Sheffield, to 57 Wicker Street where, according to the 1822 Yorkshire directory, John Leather set up as a Land Surveyor.

SAMUEL P'S BIRTH   Samuel Petty Leather was born in Sheffield in the year that George IV was crowned. The date of birth was the 8th April 1821, though this has still to be confirmed from local records.

LINES OF DESCENT   The Leathers go back to a line of the family who lived in the parishes of Burtonwood and Great

Sankey, near Warrington on the Lancashire/Cheshire border where they were farmers and shoemakers. In about 1766, George Leather, youngest son of Samuel Leather shoemaker of Great Sankey, left his home near Warrington and crossed the Pennines to settle eventually in Wakefield, where he became a distinguished colliery engineer.

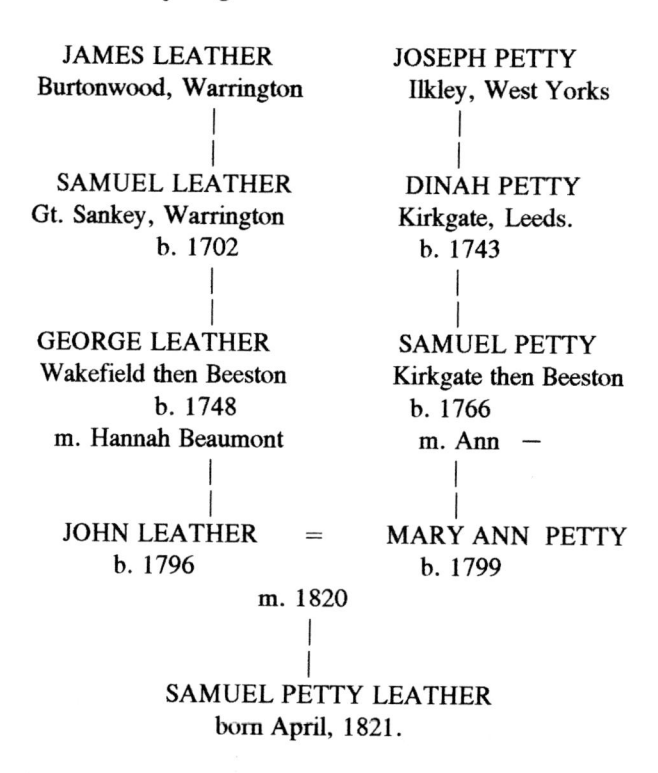

JAMES LEATHER	JOSEPH PETTY
Burtonwood, Warrington	Ilkley, West Yorks
|	|
SAMUEL LEATHER	DINAH PETTY
Gt. Sankey, Warrington	Kirkgate, Leeds.
b. 1702	b. 1743
|	|
GEORGE LEATHER	SAMUEL PETTY
Wakefield then Beeston	Kirkgate then Beeston
b. 1748	b. 1766
m. Hannah Beaumont	m. Ann —
|	|
JOHN LEATHER =	MARY ANN PETTY
b. 1796	b. 1799

m. 1820

SAMUEL PETTY LEATHER
born April, 1821.

The Pettys came from the Yorkshire Dales and can be traced to Ilkley while older generations farmed at Bolton Abbey, as long ago as 1493. It appears that, about 1765, the unmarried Dinah Petty went from Ilkley to live in Kirkgate, a street in central Leeds, to have her son Samuel, who became the baker and flour merchant of Beeston and Samuel P's grandfather. About 1812,

George Leather and his family also moved to Beeston where they had a lease on Beeston Park Colliery.

LETTER FROM MARY ANN LEATHER The following letter from Samuel P's Mother contains the first mention of him at the age of one. It also refers to the animosity which developed between his mother and his father. The letter was written to a Mrs Vitty and dated May 14th 1822, by which time Mary Ann had been married exactly two years to John and her son Samuel was almost 13 months old. She writes from Beeston, Leeds, from her parents' house which she refers to as 'home', while her husband John was working in Sheffield.

Written in beautiful, neat handwriting, folded and sealed, the letter was addressed to 'Mrs Vitty, at Mr. Joseph Shaw, Bridge Street, Sheffield'. It cost seven old pence to send (before the Penny Post) and is postmarked: LEEDS 14 MAY 1822. Just who Mrs Vitty was remains a mystery, though Joseph Shaw appears a few years later in the family history when he married Mary Ann Turner, sister of Samuel P's future wife. This is the first sign of a connection between the Leathers and the Turners. The letter is the oldest document among items of family history concerning Samuel P and is reported in full:

Dear Friend,
          You will doubtless have thought me long in writing but I thought by this to have had good news to send you, and I also hope I am likely to have a change for the best. I have been much worse since I came home than for some time before; I am very weak indeed I assure you. I think I have been on the decline for a month. I have had every means used that could be thought on and I do think the Doctor has almost been [stuck] fast with me. It has now brought on a bilious complaint or a jaundice, I am quite yellow some parts of my skin is gold colour, it has been coming on a fortnight. I have been sick nearly the day long and

loathed the sight of all sorts of food, my back is weak and I do assure you I cannot walk straight by far and after I have sat ten minuets or so I can scarcely walk at all. I can not tell whether I shall ever be well or no. I have my Brother as well as Mr Ginsburn and he seems to think me in a poor state. He was grieved past every thing when he first knew but has been very kind to me and pays the greatest attention. Oh Mrs Vitty how thankful ought I to be for the many advantages I enjoy though I have much upon my mind, yet I would be thankful to God for my many comforts. I often think if the fear of death was taken away I should be happy, that is I could give up all into the hands of my maker, and say thy will and not mine be done, I feel I am far from the fountain, but I shall trust the Lord will once more for Christ's sake shed his love abroad in my heart and make me to rejoice abundantly in him, all things below are of little value, nay I may say of no value compared to the love of God. I have suffered a great deal since I were married both in body and mind, and have been treated since I came here as though I were the falter and not him, by his friends, but I wish to be as clear of every thing as that, I do and I have felt it hard to bear, but you know the innocent often suffer instead of the guilty, so I must. John has behaved so ill to my Father as well as me that I never think of returning to him as a wife, no I feel to abhor the idea. One would have thought my affliction with rest cares of a family was sufficient without him putting us to all the trouble in his power, beside Father and Mother have almost more than they can bear, but the almighty is sufficient to help and strengthen them. It is a mercy that I have a kind sister as well as parents for I feel need of help on every side. Your Mother is over from Manchester at present at your Brother-in-law's she is pretty well and left all her friends tolerable. Mrs Vitty of Manchester is near her time of confinement, your friends here desire their kind respects and should be glad to see either you or Susannah, I feel glad I did not bring her as I am so poorly she could have had no pleasure, but if God spares me I hope to see her another spring. Samuel is very unwell at present from a bad cold or else he has improved very fast ever since we weaned him. Mother keeps a Girl to nurse and carry him out and the air does him a deal of good. Tell Susannah he can say tah! tah! and cherry tree, and can walk a little by one hand. John promised to come here on Sunday but he has never come, neither do I want him. You will be wearied of reading this long story, but I will now cut it short. Father came to your house but there was no one in, and he had not time to come again so he could not tell me how you were, but I hope you enjoy the blessing of good health, I thank you for your many favours both to me & mine, & may Almighty bless you with all things necessary both for this and for another better world. Give my love to Susannah and make my respect to your Father and Brother, our family are as well as one can expect. Mother and Sister desire me to remember them in Love to you and your family and accept the same from me.

    Your Affectionate Friend
M A Leather.
Beeston May 14th 1822.

End of letter with signature and date

Mary Ann completed the letter on the 14th May 1822 and posted it on the same day. She mentions her brother. There were three brothers, William, Samuel and John, all older than herself. Samuel and John had businesses in Hunslet, quite near to Beeston. Her sister was Eliza Petty who then would have been seventeen years old. When writing about her thirteen-month-old son Samuel, she writes: 'Mother keeps a nurse to carry him out...' so it seems that she and the baby spent much of their time at her parents' house in Beeston, rather than with her husband in Sheffield.

The date on the letter was the day before Mary Ann's second wedding anniversary yet, she says, she did not want to return to her husband 'as a wife' and tells how badly John behaved towards her parents and herself. Mary Ann talks of 'my affliction with ... cares of a family', 'John has behaved so ill to my father' and 'Father and Mother have almost more than they can bear'. There is a possible explanation for this deep animosity between husband and wife which could be due to John's discovery that his wife's father, Samuel Petty, was born illegitimate. Samuel Petty was born in 1766 in Kirkgate, Leeds, son of Dinah Petty who was not married then.

However, young Samuel P Leather seems to survive the quarrel apart from getting a bad cold. He can walk with the support of one hand, and can say 'ta ta' and 'cherry tree' which seems good progress for a thirteen-month-old baby!

THE DEATH OF SAMUEL P'S MOTHER   Three years after she wrote the letter, on the 13th May 1825, when Samuel P was four years old, Mary Ann died in Sheffield, giving birth to her second baby, who lived. She was buried at Carver Street Methodist Chapel, Sheffield on the 16th May, 1825. The fact that Mary Ann died in childbirth is recorded in JPL's red notebook. So it appears that Mary Ann did go back to her husband in Sheffield and ended her days there.

This is the first indication that Mary Ann was a Wesleyan, whereas John's family were of the established Church. A recent visit by John B and Alison Leather to the Carver Street Methodist church in Sheffield showed that the grave stones were in use as paving stones and there was no sign of that of Mary Ann Leather.

Mary Ann Leather Died May 13th 1825 Aged 26 Years – Interred May 16 1825 by J. P. Haswell

Burial record of Mary Ann Leather, aged 26

For the four-year-old Samuel P, the death of his mother was a great tragedy. He must have missed her terribly and the resulting changes in his life made a deep impression on him. His father presumably found a nurse in Sheffield to care for the boy as well as the new baby girl.

After about a year, when Samuel P was getting used to having a baby sister there came another shock for the now five-year-old Samuel. The baby girl became ill and died.

After that, Samuel P was sent back to Beeston to the home of his grandparents — Samuel and Ann Petty — where he stayed for seven years, until he was twelve years old, and where his mother's sister, Eliza Petty helped to look after him.

Samuel P's baby sister was given her mother's name, Mary Ann Leather, in her memory. The Sheffield parish records give the date of birth as the 13th May 1825, the same day as that of her mother's death. The child was baptized three months later in the Cathedral on the 10th of August. A note recording the death of Mary Ann junior is written on a scrap of paper: 'Mary Ann Leather. Died June 5th 1826, aged 13 months'. On the reverse of this slip is an advert for 'Cakes for Funerals' by a baker at 76 Wicker Street, Sheffield, which suggests that the burial did take place in Sheffield.

2 FORMATIVE YEARS

Samuel P was brought up by his maternal grandfather. The Annual Monitor for 1890 goes on to say: 'By diligent attendance at a night school, and by home study, he managed to acquire under very great difficulties, a sound education'. The Monitor is a book of appreciation of the lives of Quakers who died during the previous year. Some are just listed while other, more weighty individuals are given a paragraph or two.

Until he was twelve years old, young Samuel learned as much as he could from his grandfather, Samuel Petty, who sent him to schools in Beeston and Leeds. A copy book, written by Samuel P when he was nine or ten, reveals that, in 1830, he attended Joseph Rhodes' Seminary in Beeston, the village in which they lived. The little exercise book is decorated on each page with drawings of birds or flowers and beautifully embellished signatures. Under the heading 'Emigration' the first page states: 'Swallows are remarked for their regular departure at the approach of winter' and on the second: 'Congelation: Particles of water congealed by extreme cold make ice'. The next three pages are headed 'Flowers', 'Contentment' and 'From Shakespeare'. So it appears the boy was receiving a broad and liberal education. A second copy book is dated 1832, when Samuel P was eleven or twelve years old. The title page declares: 'Pieces written by Samuel Petty at Mr. Bewley's Academy, Leeds. 1832.' and the book ends with 'Christmas Vacation, 1832'. Samuel P must have felt more a Petty than a Leather as he uses Petty for his surname and only occasionally adds Leather to his signature.

'Penmanship', a title from ten-year-old Samuel P's copy book

Early in 1833, at the age of twelve, young Samuel was obliged to go to Liverpool to join his father, who must have already been settled there for three or four years. A letter to Samuel P from his cousin, John William Petty, written later in life in 1873, refers to 'your cousin John William who more than forty years ago was your youthful correspondent when you were located in Liverpool', suggesting Samuel P was there by 1833. This is also the date on architectural drawings of four fine Victorian houses prepared by 'Leather and Riding, Architects, Liverpool' which Samuel P must have kept throughout his life as examples of his father's work. They are beautifully drawn and portray some very fine residences, complete with butler's rooms, libraries, coach houses and stables. Each one is portrayed in plan with names of rooms and a drawing of the front elevation. The one shown has a basement with a spiral staircase in the centre of the vestibule. The ground floor has three bedrooms, a dining room, drawing room and bathroom.

One of John Leather's architect drawings of 1833

Samuel P's grandmother, Ann Petty, died in April 1835 in Beeston, the year before the following letter was written.

SAMUEL P'S LETTER FROM LIVERPOOL   Written in 1836, this letter is the strangest and most extraordinary item to have been kept in the family. It is set down in shorthand on a small piece of paper only four inches by three. Samuel P used an early type of shorthand, one year before Pittman published his shorthand in 1837. At least two people have tried to decipher the letter including JPL, who had the key to the shorthand. A second person made another partial translation in 1927 but neither completed it. Thus nobody in the family knew either who the writer of the letter was, or what was the significance of the contents until I translated it in July 1988. The result proved to be an exciting peep into Samuel P's teenage life, a period, of which we know little. He was fifteen when he wrote this letter to his grandfather in Beeston.

Samuel P's letter - actual size

By his father's second marriage Samuel P gained a step mother, Jane Kennerley who was born in Liverpool. They had six children in the ten years between 1831 and 1841 when the family lived at 55, Northumberland Street.

Samuel P refers in the letter to his step mother's child. This may have been Edward who by that time was nearly four or Mary Ann who was about eighteen months. Another daughter,

Eliza Jane was born in 1833, but it is not known if she survived as she was not with the rest of the family in the 1841 Census. In the mid 1830s, the family lived at 15 Rose Hill, less than half a mile north of Lime Street and near the beginning of Scotland Road. In those days, Liverpool was one of the biggest ports in the world and Samuel P must have had many new and exciting experiences. His urge to 'go to sea' may have been prompted by the fact that his uncle William was already starting a trading outlet in Rio de Janeiro.

Dear Grandfather,   Liverpool. May 1st 1836.

Not having received a letter from you I thought it my duty to write to you, therefore I set down this note to write and must begin my epistle with enquiring after your health, I hope you are well. I saw William before he went to Rio Janeiro and was glad to see him, and my uncle received cloth you sent him which was soon popped up the spout. Since my last letter to you I am quite unsettled in my mind what with the state of father's affairs and other family matters. I think I shall never spend my time here. Dear Grandfather, it is now I want your advice, I shall be glad if you will advise me what to do. My stepmother and me do not agree nor can I please her whatever I do. If I laid my life at her disposal she would not be satisfied; and my father being quite under her control, whatever she says or does is right. From the state of my father's affairs I think his business will not last long. My father has agreed with his creditors to meet their demands in six months which is nearly expired and then I do not know which way he will turn alas. I shall never learn the business from my father being naturally under her control. I must do what she tells me and so am to obey to her call and command. I have to nurse her child all day while she is galloping up and down after him as the persons he is to transact business with. As my father is naturally governed by her, he can not go across the water but she is at his tail. I am now learning to nurse instead of surveying under stiff circumstances. I write to you to give me your advice. I am come to the determination not to stop [here]. I want your opinion then I will acquaint my father. I would like to go to sea, why with your influence I might get a good place but your advice would decide and matter very [much]. I can not stop here any longer, I have no pocket money. I can not get any money or I would have come to you before now. Dear Grandfather, what fair conclusion you come to let me know as soon as possible. If you think I should do best at sea as I think I should, let me know. If you think I should do better some other way let me know. I must now draw to a close for morning is dawning and I must shut up.

S. P. L.

The 'William' mentioned in the letter was William Petty, SPL's uncle and Samuel Petty's eldest son, who later started the South American end of the family business of 'Brazil [cloth] Merchants and Shipping Agents'. 'Popped up the spout' indicates the gift of cloth was taken to the pawnbroker's. Going 'across the water' is crossing the River Mersey to Birkenhead. In spite of his obviously unhappy situation and his entreaties to his grandfather, Samuel P remained with his father and family in Liverpool until 1838, when he was eighteen.

JOHN LEATHER'S LIVERPOOL FAMILY   During those years, the Leather family lived in Rose Hill, while John had his architect's office nearly a mile away at 6 Clarendon Rooms, South John Street, near the docks. Samuel P trained as an apprentice with his father during this time and worked in the office, learning the basics of surveying, draughtsmanship and design which was to stand him in good stead later on. Over the next twenty-five years John Leather's family lived in eight different houses, mostly in the Toxteth Park area. In spite of the problems referred to in the above letter, John's business seemed to thrive. In 1843 his office transferred to Tarleton Street then in

1847 the business was 'Leather and Hosking' of the more upmarket Dale Street and finally from 1849 to 1859 the architect business moved into offices in prestigious Lime Street.

Although John Leather's life as an architect appears successful enough from these references, which are taken from Liverpool directories of the time, he does not appear to have been the designer of any notable buildings or features of the Liverpool skyline and most of his work must have been of an ordinary, bread-and-butter nature.

John Leather's Liverpool family included two boys and four girls. But later in life, he must have been a sad father. On a January day in 1850, his eldest son, Edward, only eighteen years old, was found drowned in the River Mersey, a likely suicide, and this must have shaken not only John but the whole of the family. His second son became a carpenter and married Elizabeth Sutton, daughter of a steward. Two of the girls married, one to a carpenter, and a third may have died young.

MACLEA AND MARCH OF LEEDS   At the age of eighteen, Samuel P left Liverpool and returned to Leeds where from 1839 to 1842 he was apprenticed, by his grandfather, to a firm of mechanical engineers and machine makers, Maclea and March of Leeds. This was a firm of brass and iron founders who manufactured flax machinery and hydraulic presses, based at Union Foundry on Dewsbury Road. During this three year period he lived with his grandfather in Beeston, less than a mile away. The Annual Monitor for 1890 states: 'and though this occupation was not congenial to him, he fulfilled his term of service, and at the same time, as opportunity served, pursued his studies with avidity.' Working in an iron foundry added another dimension to Samuel P's practical training, where he no doubt learned pattern making, casting, turning and finishing and the use of metals. At the end of this period he was ready to take on anything in the engineering world.

THE 1841 CENSUS   This is the first census of any real use to those interested in family history. It lists every person in every household by name, approximate age (to the nearest 5 years), sex and occupation. It also notes whether or not the persons were born in the same county, though it does not give exact addresses. In the Leeds census returns, Samuel Petty's household is recorded next to Beeston Hall. It lists who spent the night of the 7th June 1841 and shows Samuel P Leather, who was in fact just twenty years old, living with his grandfather Samuel Petty, then seventy-five. Three years later, old Samuel Petty died at the home of his servant Mary Wilson.

[Near Beeston Hall] Beeston, Leeds, Yorkshire.

Name	Age	Occupation	Born Yorks
Samuel Petty	75	independent	Yes
Samuel Leather	20	machine maker	Yes
Mary Wilson	25	F.S. [female servant]	No

On that same day, over in Liverpool, John Leather's family were gathered, though one, Eliza Jane, is absent:

[55] Northumberland Street, Toxteth Park, Liverpool.

Name	Age	Occupation	Born Yorks
John Leather	45	architect	No (not born Lancashire)
Jane Leather	40		Yes
Edward Leather	9		Yes
Mary Ann Leather	6		Yes
Victoria Leather	4		Yes
George Leather	2		Yes
Hannah Leather	3 mos		Yes

A JOB WITH UNCLE GEORGE LEATHER   On the 1st November 1842, Samuel P started work with the Leeds Waterworks Company under George Leather, his uncle and his father's older brother. At this time George Leather had an office at Springfield House, Infirmary Gardens, Wellington Street, Leeds where he was in partnership with his son John Wignall Leather. The business was described as Geo Leather and Son, Civil Engineers and Land Agents.

In the 1820s, George Leather was Engineer for the Aire and Calder Navigation Company and was employed on the construction of the Goole Canal, from Knottingley to the River Ouse at Goole (opened 1826), as well as Goole Docks and the lock gates there. In 1827, he published plans for the 'Aire and Calder Navigation' a series of cuts and canals from Wakefield and Leeds to Ferrybridge.

The seven foot Aire and Calder Canal was subsequently built and included many bridges and culverts, the docks at Leeds and the magnificent cast iron aqueduct at Stanley Ferry, near Wakefield, which in a single span of 155 feet carries the canal high over the River Calder, a lasting memorial to the engineering ability of George Leather who was also the designer and engineer of six other bridges, only two of which still exist today: the stone Crown Point Bridge and the iron Victoria Bridge both of which span the River Aire in central Leeds.

In 1842, George Leather was chief engineer to the Leeds corporation waterworks when he took on Samuel P to work with the company. Samuel P's job description is: 'Superintendent of the outdoor works of the Leeds Waterworks Company.' It was at this time that George Leather and Son were involved in the large Eccup storage reservoir scheme, for the supply of water to the city of Leeds, so it is likely that Samuel P spent much of the next six years in this area, north of the city. It was a big scheme to be working on and involved outdoor survey work, engineering problems concerned with the building of the Eccup dam and a 1¼ mile long tunnel through the Alwoodley ridge, pipe-laying and the construction of open water channels.

The scheme is described as one of the earliest of its kind with a 50 acre reservoir at Eccup, a second reservoir at Weetwood and a service reservoir at Woodhouse Moor.

Eccup Reservoir today

In a letter, dated the 14th May 1843, from George Leather to his daughter Maria, there is mention of Sam, referring to Samuel P himself, as follows:

> 'I have received Sam's letter, and some fish came before it. Tell him if he likes to shoot Rooks he may have a day at Temple Newsome on Tuesday. I shot 26 yesterday with a rifle and got 24 of them, the other two dropped into nests. Tom Philips will attend him and find him a rifle and ammunition. He may take one or two with him if he likes.'

THE DEATH OF SAMUEL PETTY SPL's grandfather died on the 6th August 1844 at the fine age of seventy-eight. The death certificate gives the place of death as 9 Green Mount Place, Holbeck, with Mary Wilson present at the death at the same address. In his advancing years, when he could no longer look after himself, old Samuel Petty may have gone to live with his servant Mary Wilson, in the neighbouring village of Holbeck. Samuel Petty's son, Samuel Petty, junior, had become prominent in the manufacture of earthenware at the Hunslet Hall Pottery, south Leeds.

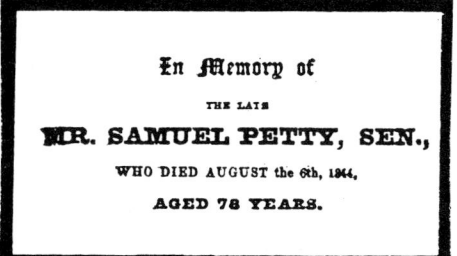

> In Memory of
> THE LATE
> **MR. SAMUEL PETTY, SEN.,**
> WHO DIED AUGUST the 6th, 1844,
> AGED 78 YEARS.

The relationship between Samuel P and his grandfather had been a long and close one. Samuel Petty had looked after young Samuel and cared for him since he was born. He had been a father figure to him and his death must have been a sad occasion for the young man whose life was quickly changing.

Samuel P was now an independent young gentleman, an experienced surveyor, draughtsman and engineer. He had been with Leeds waterworks for some eighteen months, was twenty-three years old and his future was bright.

After his grandfather died, Samuel P went to live at Knostrop New Hall for a year or so, the home of his uncle George Leather. Knostrop was a small village on the south side of Leeds and a mile or so from Beeston. In 1958 Knostrop New Hall was part of Lord Halifax's Temple Newsham estate. Twenty years later it was demolished to make way for a power station.

3 MARRIAGE

AN EARLY PHOTOGRAPH   It was 1845 and things were looking brighter for Samuel P. He was well settled in his first job as Inspector of Waterworks in Leeds, had probably already met Jane Anne Turner, the girl who was to become his wife. It was then that he arranged to have his photograph taken!

The result was a 2½ by 2 inch seated portrait mounted in a red leather case. The date 1845, is written under the photograph — a Daguerreotype, invented by the Frenchman Daguerre and patented in 1839, so this is an early example. Subjects had to sit still for 40 seconds or so and the result can look like a negative or a positive depending on the angle. The photograph was made on a layer of silver on a copper plate with a frame and glass cover, the whole thing being sealed and mounted in a case.

Samuel P Leather age 24

HOW SAMUEL MET JANE   The letter from Mary Ann Leather to Mrs. Vitty shows that the Pettys knew Joseph Shaw of Sheffield back in 1822. Joseph Shaw later married Mary Ann Turner, Noah and Harriet Turner's eldest daughter. Thus the Pettys must have come to know of the Turner family. The Turners lived in Masbrough, Rotherham until the mid 1820s, when they moved to south Leeds, to Hunslet, where their last two children were baptised and where, in 1826, Noah was a 'foreman' and lived in Jack Lane, Hunslet.

The village of Hunslet was not far from Beeston and was also the location of the pottery in which Samuel Petty had an interest. In 1834 Noah Turner's name appeared in the Leeds Directory: 'Noah Turner, flint glass manufacturer, 65 Central Market, Leeds.' In the same directory Samuel Petty is given as both 'baker and flour dealer' and on a different page as 'earthenware manufacturer'. The two families had a common interest in business. By 1837 the Turner family had returned to Rotherham where Noah Turner remained until his death in 1853. Samuel P may have met Jane and the Turner family in his childhood days and he renewed her acquaintance after he had established himself in his first job in Leeds.

MARRIAGE   On the 22nd September 1846, when Samuel P was twenty-five years old, a wedding took place in Rotherham parish church. Samuel Petty Leather was married to Miss Jane Anne Turner, youngest daughter of Noah and Harriet Turner. Noah was born in Brierley Hill, Staffordshire in 1785 and married Harriet Glaizebrook in Rotherham in the same Church in March, 1807. Their daughter Jane Anne was the eighth child of the family and was born on the 27th July 1825, and baptised in Hunslet, Leeds. She was four years younger than Samuel P and 21 years of age when the wedding took place. The certificate of marriage shows Jane Anne's older sister Hannah to be a witness. Where was Noah?

SETTING UP HOUSE   On the 19th September 1846, Samuel P visited Thomas Dale's furniture store in Barnsley, a good eighteen miles south of Leeds, and purchased a large collection of household items for his new home at number 4 Sheepscar Place, North Street, Leeds. The bill came to £103-0-11 and was posted on to him at Sheepscar Place 10 days later on the 29th September. This considerable amount of money must have represented at least twice his annual salary at the time. It is possible that Samuel P had been left some money (perhaps by his grandfather?).

The household articles Samuel P bought included the following amazing collection of items:

6 Ecarte chairs 24/-	£7 - 4 - 0
Spring Sofa	7 - 10 - 0
Dining Table with sp leaf	9 - 0 - 0
22 Yds of Marble Carpet 3/-	3 - 6 - 0
19¼ Yds of Drab & Blue Carpet 2/9	2 - 12 - 0
Hearth Rug	0 - 12 - 0
4 Post Bedstead and Cornice	10 - 10 - 0
Palliasse 16/-, soft -do- 28/-	2 - 4 - 0
Feather Bed 5.5.0. B & sp 2/-	6 - 6 - 0
French Bedstead 4ft 6	2 - 2 - 0
Mattress to -do-	0 - 18 - 6
Flock Bed and Bolster	1 - 10 - 0
2 feather pillows	0 - 12 - 6
Pair of Bedroom Tables	1 - 6 - 0
Swing Glass [mirror] & marble tray	2 - 10 - 0
11½ Yds Stair Carpet 1/5	0 - 16 - 5½
Window Pole and Rings	0 - 10 - 6
Pair Bedroom Tables	3 - 12 - 0

Bronze Fender 21/- Fire Irons 13/6	1 - 14 - 6
Birch Rocking Chair	1 - 16 - 0
6 Cane Chairs 6/6	1 - 19 - 0
Kitchen Table	0 - 16 - 0
Kitchen Fender and Fire Irons	0 - 10 - 6
Easy Chair	5 - 0 - 0
Set of Duck Bed Curtains	6 - 15 - 0
Set of Window Curtains	1 - 18 - 6
Wing Wardrobe	8 - 8 - 0
11 Yds Blue Carpet 2/9	1 - 10 - 3
1 coconut Mat	0 - 1 -10
2 Yds ¾ Oil Cloth 4/4	0 - 4 - 4
17 21" Stair Rods. 3 doz Eyes	0 - 7 - 8
2 Pairs Blanket 21/-, 1 Pr 14/-	2 - 16 - 0
Paid Debt for Carriage of Goods	0 - 18 - 0
Men 1 Day & Expense fixing Goods	1 - 2 - 6
	£103 - 0 -11

Sheepscar Place no longer exists but is given in the Leeds directory for 1847 where, among a list of six related Leathers, is: 'Samuel Petty Leather, Inspector of Waterworks, 4 Sheepscar Place, Leeds.' However, the directory for 1849, two years later, gives Samuel P's address as 'Knostrop', the home of his Uncle George Leather. There seems to be no explanation as to why he gave up his newly furnished home at Sheepscar Place, north of the city centre, to return to Knostrop. Perhaps his wife was already showing signs of illness and had to return to her family.

A NEW POST IN MANCHESTER   On the 22nd January 1849, Samuel P began as 'Foreman over a portion of the works of the Manchester Corporation Waterworks, under Mr J F Bateman'. This was a position he held for over three years until May 1852. In Leeds, Samuel P may have already met Mr Bateman, who was a consultant hired by the Leeds waterworks company. In

Manchester, Mr J F Bateman, an eminent civil engineer, was in charge of the construction of the Manchester waterworks at Woodhead. He was at one time President of the Institution of Civil Engineers.

Samuel P's new home in Manchester was 1 Churchill Terrace, Everton Road, Chorlton upon Medlock, south east of the city.

DEATH OF JANE ANNE LEATHER   On the 16th January 1852, at number 1 Churchill Terrace, Jane Anne died. She was only 26 years old and there were no children. The cause of death is given as 'indigestion 4 months and apoplexy 24 hours'. The certificate gives Samuel P's occupation as 'Surveyor'. The loss of his young wife must have been devastating for him. He had been married for over 5 years and was now well established in his employment and in his home. This was the second great tragedy of his life and once again the future for him must have looked bleak. Jane was buried in Ardwick Cemetery, south Manchester. On the burial certificate, the address of the cemetery is given as: 'Ford Road, near the entrance of the Gorton New Road.' The cemetery no longer exists.

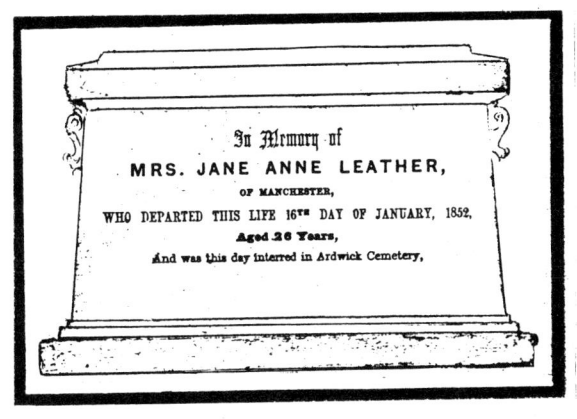

> In Memory of
> MRS. JANE ANNE LEATHER,
> OF MANCHESTER,
> WHO DEPARTED THIS LIFE 16TH DAY OF JANUARY, 1852,
> Aged 26 Years,
> And was this day interred in Ardwick Cemetery,

Funeral Card for Jane Anne Leather

TO STOCKPORT WATERWORKS   On the 28th May 1852, Samuel P left his job with Manchester Corporation and started work with Stockport Waterworks Company, where he was Water Engineer, a position which he held for over three years until March 1855. The new address in Stockport was 10 Little Moor. Today Little Moor is not a street but an area of Stockport.

A CHANGE OF PRONUNCIATION   At some time during his life, Samuel P changed the pronunciation of his surname from the usual Leather, rhyming with feather, to Lea-ther, rhyming with 'leader'. The descendants of Samuel P have often wondered why this happened. Some have tried to change the pronunciation back again without much success. In order to change one's name easily there must not only be a good reason for doing so but there must be particular circumstances in which it can be carried out. For example, it is much easier to do this for a person moving to a new part of the country, starting a new job and meeting new friends.

Such circumstances may have come about at this time and prompted Samuel P to make the change. The death of his young wife must have left him feeling lonely and isolated. Since he had already lived in Lancashire as a teenager in Liverpool, and as he had acquired the post in Manchester through contacts with his uncle, the move across the Pennines may not have been a great wrench, but it did distance him physically from the Leather family in Yorkshire, particularly from his uncle George .

It was in 1852 that the Bilberry Dam collapsed. The dam, in the Holme Valley, near Huddersfield — for which George Leather was chief engineer — had been built eight years previously, but was never watertight. Its failure in the middle of the night on the 5th February brought the worst possible of disasters. Eighty-one people were killed and the floodwaters left a train of devastation to mills, dyehouses, bridges, workshops, cottages, public houses and churches in the industrial and populated valley below. George Leather's brilliant career came sharply to an end. The occurrence of this catastrophe may have added the final reason for Samuel P's wish to start afresh with a new name. It may have even encouraged him to enter the gas industry when the time came.

However, he did not cut himself off altogether from the Yorkshire Leathers as, thirty years later, his cousin John Wignall Leather (George's son), supported him in his application to become an associate member of the Institution of Civil Engineers. He did seem to drift away from his own father and he may have wished to remove himself from his unhappy memories of Liverpool, his step mother and her family. He kept no letters from his father nor is there any mention of his father or relatives from Liverpool, except for an aunt Bennett in a letter dated 1868, and the four architectural drawings.

This sense of isolation, along with a new job in Stockport, a new house, a new wife and a new home must have been like a fresh start in life to Samuel, which needed to be recognised by something as radical as a new pronunciation of his name. He must have thought the new name an improvement, perhaps to the extent of sounding 'posher' than the old one. One must remember, too, that he called himself just Samuel Petty until he was twelve years old and therefore was not strongly attached to his family name.

Samuel P now seemed to have tremendous confidence in himself and his future. He was a self-made man and must have felt in charge of his own destiny. In spite of the loss of his wife, he was able to rise up above the tragedy with great strength, and to see clearly where he was going. From available evidence, there was no dramatic split or rift or argument within the family, but only what was a fresh start for him in a new period of his life.

SECOND MARRIAGE   On the 17th February 1853, at the age of 31, Samuel P married Hannah Turner, daughter of Noah and Harriet Turner and older sister of Jane Anne, his deceased wife. The wedding took place in the Unitarian Church, Saint Peter's Square, Stockport and the couple were married 'according to the Rites and Ceremonies of the English Presbyterians'. Hannah, seven years older than Samuel, was born in Rotherham in 1814. Stockport was already Samuel P's home town which was one reason for the location of the wedding there. Hannah's father, Noah Turner, was not a witness at the wedding and may not have been well enough to travel to Stockport. He died two months later and was buried at Rotherham Parish Church in April 1853. The reason for the wedding taking place in the Unitarian Church was due to a rule in the Church of England Prayer Book which prevents a man from marrying his deceased wife's sister.

By the last day of 1853, Hannah gave birth to a baby boy and Tom Turner Leather was born at 10 Little Moor Stockport on the 31st December 1853. 'Tom' was a new name in the family and 'Turner' was Hannah's maiden name.

During his time in Stockport, Samuel P was called in to an engineering problem at the gasworks in the nearby town of Hyde where a gas tank was leaking and which had to be made water tight. He successfully accomplished the task and at the same time paved the way for his future employment in the town.

PAGES TORN FROM A DIARY   Five pages have been preserved from Samuel P's diary for 1855. They cover four weeks in which Samuel P left his job in Stockport and took up his first post in the gas industry. From the number of burst pipes he had to deal with at the end of February and beginning of March, the thought may have occurred to him that maybe gas pipes had fewer problems! Perhaps the more complex gas industry had a more challenging future. It is interesting to see that, in amongst all the notes on his working days, including Saturdays and even a Sunday, there is the underlined phrase: 'Fun at Theatre'. At least Samuel P enjoyed some leisure time when he could get it.

February 26 Monday 1855. Pipes burst at Nos 23 & 26, Bentley.
March 2 Friday. Burst behind No. 18 Wellington Road North.
March 3 Saturday. Cleaned new filter. Henry Marsland's men.
March 6 Tuesday. At Hyde to see Mr. Haigh.
March 8 Thursday. Piece blown out of pipe in Wellington Road North. Turned water into No.1 Filter and took off unfiltered water. (Fun at Theatre)
March 9 Friday. Men at work all last night Great Portwood Street. 3 inch Valve broken completely by frost. Mr H Marsland's men commenced at Great Portwood Street today at Noon (5 men) pumping main blown joint.
March 10 Saturday. Piece of metal blown out in N B Lane and also York Street Portwood near Ashton Paints W R South.
March 12 Monday. Bolt broken at pedestal of No 1 pump at ½ past 10 yesterday morning. Completed, and pump at work by 10 o-clock at night (Sunday) Saw Mr Darwen respecting Hyde.
March 13 Tuesday. Received letter from Joseph Hibbert of Hyde to meet Hyde (Directors) Gas Company next Monday evening.
March 14 Wednesday. Mr Gowenlock commenced for the S.W.W.Co this morning. He is to take charge of W...? & filters and I am to manage the rest of the Works.
March 16 Friday. Burst pipe near Mr Lisstrot, Brinksway. Burst pipe near to Mr Brooks, Brinksway.
March 17 Saturday. Burst pipe No 5 Berry's Buildings Castle St.
March 19 Monday. Attending meeting of Gas Directors, Hyde. Appointed Resident Engineer at a Salary of 100.
March 20 Tuesday. At Leeds to see Mr Horsfall, £10 to be paid within 10 days of this time.
March 21 Wednesday. Fast Day. Last day of Engagement with the Stockport Water Works Company. Received from Mr Darwen, 3 plans & specifications.

SAMUEL P ENTERS THE GAS INDUSTRY   On the 22nd March 1855, Samuel P started work as Resident Engineer of the Hyde Gasworks Company at a salary of £100 a year. The gasworks were situated at Millwood on Alfred Street, next to the Peak Forest Canal. The diary entries include the first few days of his career in this new field. It shows that he had much more responsibility in his new post and probably gained more satisfaction from being in such a position. Samuel P later became manager of the company.

March 22 Thursday. Started at Hyde with my Engagement with Gas Co. Copied the Inventory of Mr Booths Gas Works, Pipes &c.
March 23 Friday. All morning on the New Works by Canal Side. Went with Mr. Darwin to Mr. Booth's Works. Accompanied Mr Booth over his Works to get information over the New Works.
March 24 Saturday. Examining the plans & specifications &c of the New Works. Looking over the old Works.
March 26 Monday. Taking the metres. 267 is the No of consumers including some of the weekly Tennants. Attending meeting of Directors. 20 tons of Slack cannel [coal] order. Glancy engaged for fortnight at 16/-, Daniels at 15/-, Bennett at 30/-.
March 27 Tuesday. 100 light meters came this morning. Bennett will not start unless engaged for 6 months. Redfern brought better than 4 tons of the slack cannel which we shall be unable to use. Must be a mistake. Writing specification for chimney.
March 28 Wednesday. At Old Works this morning to try the slack. Meeting of Directors, the second best cannel to be used. To see Mr. Haig to bear half expense of the Road as far as his land. Obliged to draw the charges of slack cannel. Arranged for 2 retorts every 3 hrs.

A NEW HOME IN HYDE   The Leathers lived in Kingston Brow on Manchester Road, Hyde for over eight years from 1855 to 1863. Kingston is an area on the north side of Manchester Road and not far from the gasworks. Samuel P was not only the resident engineer but also soon became the manager of the Hyde gasworks.

On December 2nd 1859, at Kingston Brow, Hyde, John Petty Leather was born. He was Samuel and Hannah's second son. John is named after Samuel's father, John Leather and Samuel's mother's maiden name Petty is not forgotten. When Hannah had John Petty she was already 45 years old. Tom was then six.

The death of Hannah's mother, Harriet Turner, came on the 29th January 1857, at Greasbrough Lane, Greasbrough, Rotherham at the age of seventy-one. Harriet is shown as the widow of Noah Turner, Glass Blower. William Raybould, Olivia Turner's husband was in attendance at the death at the same address. It is possible that this was the Raybould's home and that Harriet was living there with her daughter's family. The Census of 1861 for the Rotherham area shows the Raybould family here with thirty-year-old Willam Raybould working as a stove grate fitter. His wife Olivia is also thirty and two of their daughters are Eliza aged three and Alice Jane aged two.

INTEREST IN QUAKERISM   While in Stockport Hannah began to attend the Friends Meeting there. After moving to Hyde it is said that she and her son Tom walked several miles each way to Meeting. The Annual Monitor goes on to relate:

> "On returning home one First-Day, little Tom, climbing up on his father's knee, asked him, 'Papa when are you going to go with us to Meeting?' This so touched the father that he yielded himself to the loving appeal, and afterwards became a diligent attender of Meetings for Worship; thus fulfilling the Scripture

declaration, 'A little child shall lead them.' He [Samuel P] had before this been accustomed to attend meetings on special occasions when ministering Friends from a distance were announced to be present; and though he seldom spoke to others of his religious experience, he looked back to ministry which he heard on some of these occasions as having been instrumental in his conversion."

The photograph of Tom, aged about seven, shows him standing out of doors, perhaps for better light conditions, but because he had to stand still for several seconds, he is supported by a chair behind him and is holding on to something that looks like a fishing rod.

Tom Turner Leather, age 7.

TOM GOES AWAY TO SCHOOL
Tom was sent to Penketh School, a Quaker preparatory school near Warrington. This was only a stone's throw from Great Sankey where his great grandfather George Leather (senior) was born. Tom wrote the following letter home at the tender age of eight. Young Tom is feeling the time dragging and his thoughts are very much with his home and parents. In fact he is home sick and cannot wait for the end of term.

Penketh School
4th mo 30th 1862

My dear parents,
I have been expecting a letter from you every day but now it is monthly letters. We shall break up in about 6 weeks. Mr. Crighton took us a walk this week along the River Mersey and I very much liked it.
Please write soon. With love
I remain Your affectionate T. T. Leather

In March 1860, Samuel P had another photograph taken with a photographer in Manchester (A. Brothers, 14 St. Ann's Square, Manchester). This time it was of much clearer definition with tinted flesh tones. By 1860, the Daguerreotype had largely been replaced by the collodion positive, of which this is an example. The photograph was made by a 'thin' negative on glass and backed by black, to form a positive and was in use between 1852 and the 1870s.

Samuel P Leather age 39

The photograph was given a decorative mask with a cover glass and fitted in a small case. The photographs of Tom and Hannah (see next page) were taken round about the same time.

SAMUEL P BECOMES A FREEMASON   In January 1858, Samuel P was received into Masonry, into Fidelity Lodge and Industry Lodge in Hyde. Over the next ten years he took an active part, receiving certificates of 'Templar Knight Companion', 'Red Cross of Babylon' and 'Knight Templar Priest' etc.

PHOTOGRAPH OF HANNAH
The seated portrait of Hannah shows her in a beautiful patterned dress. Similar photographs in the National Museum of Photography in Bradford are dated 1860 and have the same gilded masks and frames, mounted in plush lined cases. Hannah was 46 years old when this photograph was taken. The rather severe stare was due to the fact that subjects had to sit very still for several seconds.

CENSUS OF 1861   The Census for Hyde not only records the whole of Samuel P's family but also a niece he is employing as a servant. Anna Mary was the daughter of Hannah's sister Harriet who was married to Samuel Bennett.

Address: Manchester Road, Hyde, Cheshire.
Samuel Petty Leather Head mar 39 Manager Gasworks, b. Sheffield
Hannah Leather   Wife   mar 46   Rotherham, Yorks.
Tom Turner   Leather Son 7 Scholar   Stockport, Ches.
John Leather   Son 10mo   Hyde, Cheshire.
Anna Mary Bennett   Niece unm. 15 Servant Otley, Yorks.

4 THE FAMILY IN BURNLEY

On the 31st July 1863, Samuel P moved house with his family to Burnley in Lancashire to take up his duties as Manager and Chief Engineer of the Burnley Corporation Gas Department. The new address was The Gas Works, Burnley and the house was situated at the junction of Saunder Bank and Coke Street, right at the entrance to the works.

   The gas business was founded in 1823 as the Burnley Gaslight Company and taken over by the corporation in 1854. Lane Bridge gasworks were situated in an angle of the Leeds-Liverpool Canal with the small River Calder on the north side. The canal is elevated on a sixty foot high embankment with an aqueduct over the river. There was access to coal barges on the canal and the coal was transferred directly into the works. By 1863, the gasworks were forty years old and ready for some expansion and modernisation.

   When Samuel P first visited the works after his appointment, a strange sight greeted him. At that time, the coal was carried from the canal on an overhead jinny rail, the conveyor being driven by a steam engine which ran at an enormous speed, much quicker than it should have done. Consequently, a very high pressure had to be maintained when the engine was working. When Samuel P arrived he found Mr King, the Borough Accountant, sitting on the safety valve of the steam boiler to get the pressure up!

ANOTHER LETTER FROM TOM   The boys Tom and John were at this stage nine and three years old respectively. On the 10th June 1864, Tom Turner Leather sent a letter home from school. It was written when he was ten, in neat copperplate handwriting:

> Penketh School.
> 10 mo 6th 1864.
>
> Dear Parents,
> I now write these few lines to you hoping to find you all very well. I received the letter which you sent me. Is John Smith well? The Committee are to examine tomorrow we expect. How are they getting on with the Gas Holder? Have they got any part of the wall done yet. I send my love to you all. I remain your
> affectionate son
> T.T.Leather.

That Christmas, Tom was allowed to spend the holiday at home though normally, it seems, there was no such thing as a school holiday at the festive season. The following year, Christmas 1865, Samuel P wrote to the Head of Penketh School asking if Tom could be at home again over the holiday and received a rather formal reply turning down the suggestion. The letter stated that the Master could not grant applications for pupils leaving school at Christmas but that this was up to the Committee who 'by all means wish to avoid something like a Christmas Vacation.' A post script to the letter said that Tom was very well and improving in his studies and 'he is thinking of writing thee a long letter next week'! Samuel P was angry that his son could not spend Christmas with the family.

In any case, he did not send John to Penketh School, (though John's son, Arnold attended in later years). John first attended a day school in Burnley, from the age of four until he was seven

(1864-67), a school kept by Miss Morston in Hargreaves Street, just three or four blocks from the gasworks. In 1867, John went to a preparatory school in Egremont, near Whitehaven in Cumbria.

PROGRESS AT THE WORKS   Under Samuel P's new management, the gasworks developed rapidly, expanding on all fronts to cope with the increased demand for gas, for street lighting as well as for home lighting. Samuel P himself made the drawings and designs and drew up estimates for the necessary extensions and improvements carried out on the works. He also acted as overseer to the new construction work. In his letter, Tom asked about the river retaining wall which was being built and how the building of a new gas holder was progressing. It was a boom time for Burnley's gas industry as, in the next nineteen years — until 1882 — Samuel P erected one large retort house, two purifying houses, four gas holder tanks and five gas holders, two of which were triple lifts. Gas production was continually being increased to satisfy the demand of a fast increasing population.

THE DEATH OF HANNAH'S BROTHER   In February 1865, John Turner, son of Noah and brother of Hannah, died while staying at an inn in Nottingham. He was 50 years old. A letter to Hannah from her nephew Arthur C Turner (John Turner's son) describes the event. Arthur C Turner lived in Swinton near Rotherham. It is possible that John Turner was visiting the Westerman family, relations who lived in Nottingham at that time. The Westermans later came to live in Burnley where James Henry Westerman had a job at the gasworks and where, in 1881, he was chief mechanic in charge of gas stoking. He was the nephew of Samuel P. The letter to Hannah follows.

       Swinton.
      Feb. 16th 1865.
Dear Aunt,
  It is now scarce six weeks since you saw your brother my dear father, then in good health and strength and in high spirits, and now in deep grief, I have to acquaint you with his death.
  My dear Father was on a journey and on Tuesday night, while at Nottingham he suddenly expired in the Commercial Room of the inn where he was staying.
  This is a severe blow to us all. My dear mother especially feels her bereavement very acutely. She has been very ill ever since. Mrs Shaw has been down here today, perhaps she will write to you. Excuse me not writing before, I feel I have only to plead my grief as an excuse.
  We inter my dear father at 11 o'clock on Saturday morning.
  Hoping Mr Leather and your sons are all well.
     I remain,
     Yours faithfully
     A C Turner.

  As yet we don't know who John Turner's wife was. Mrs Shaw was Hannah's oldest sister, the wife of Joseph Shaw and lived in Sheffield.

JOHN GOES TO SCHOOL IN EGREMONT In July 1867, at the tender age of seven, John Petty Leather was sent away to boarding school, quite the done thing in those days. He went to Aldborough House Preparatory School, a Quaker establishment in Church Street, Egremont, near Whitehaven in Cumbria. The school was kept by Miss Martha Ecroyd Smith and on the 5th October, the same year, Samuel P received a quarterly bill for expenses and a school report on his son. John was in the third class which had only four pupils.

ALDBRO' HOUSE PREPARATORY SCHOOL

Samuel Leather   Dr. to M E Smith
Quarter ending 5th of 10th month 1867:

Board and instruction to John Leather	£8 - 8 - 0
Washing 12/- Drilling 3/6	15 - 6
Use of Books 1/6 Stationery. 3/6	5 - 0
Lesson Books 4/6	4 - 6
Excursions and ferry 2/6	2 - 6
Pocket money 1/-	1 - 0
Medicine 6d Hairdresser 6d	1 - 0
	£19 - 17 - 6

JOHN P LEATHER'S FIRST SCHOOL REPORT

Quarterly Register.   John Leather   Oct 3rd 1867.
Average value for Lessons 41
Highest attainable 50   Class Position 2nd
Third Class. 4 pupils.

Reading 2nd	Writing 1st	Spelling 2nd
History 3rd	Geography 3rd	Arithmetic 1st

Mental Arithmetic 2nd
General improvement for the first Quarter satisfactory, and conduct very good.

John wrote home from Aldborough School and one letter which he sent at the age of seven he describes as a 'quarterly letter' which seems a long time for the parents to wait for news. He also notes that 'There are 23 boys in the school, five constant boarders and two weekly boarders.' In May 1868, John writes to say there will be six weeks' holiday from the 26th June. In the same letter he writes: 'Miss Wheeler took us out to get some oak for Royal Oak day and we got a good deal. We intended to make an ark of oak but we did not. We have been reading a very nice book called *The Golden Thread.'*

John was also in correspondence with George Willey, presumably the young son of George Collisson Willey who died at the age of thirty-seven in 1864. There seems to be a relationship here, but just what it is, is uncertain. A possibility is that George Willey (senior) was married to Sarah Turner, and that would make sense of the references in this letter to John as 'cousin' and his parents as 'uncle and aunt'. Cousin Farrar must be the grandson of Mary Ann and Joseph Shaw, since the Shaw's eldest daughter, Sarah, married Abraham Farrar. Hubert Collisson must be a relation of the Willeys:

Western Bank, 1868.
My dear John,
                I was very glad that you had written to Grandmama. I read your letter and I shall be glad if you will come and stay with us a week or two.

Give my love to Tom, Uncle and Aunt. Write and tell me when you come. Jane and I went to Bradford last Tuesday. Cousin Farrar has been over to see us and is going to a tutor at Northampton to learn to talk so as we can understand him. Tell me how much gas you have been making this winter. Hubert Collisson and Arthur Haye send their love to you. Believe me your affectionate Cousin.
                Geo Willey.

HANNAH'S LIFE IN BURNLEY Hannah had already started to attend Quaker meetings soon after she was married, while living at Hyde, and continued her connection with the Society of Friends by attending meetings at Marsden. She regularly walked from Burnley up the hill to the Friends Meeting House in Marsden, both on Sundays and during the week. She also attended Quaker business meetings in Bolton and at

Crawshawbooth (in Rossendale) and other towns within the Marsden Monthly Meeting.

During the 1860s, Hannah was very active in visiting the poor in Burnley and helping people in many ways. Near to the gasworks, which was in an old part of the town, there were several streets of poor back-to-back houses. She had a school for women at her own house for a few years, where she taught sewing, reading and 'other necessary learning of that description, which they were not already possessed of.'

SAMUEL P JOINS THE SOCIETY OF FRIENDS Samuel P was baptized into the Church of England. His father and family were of the established Church, though his mother was a Wesleyan. Samuel P's first marriage was in the Parish Church Rotherham and his second marriage, in the Unitarian Church in Stockport; and now he had decided to join the Quakers! It seems likely that Hannah had already joined Friends and that Samuel P was quite familiar with Quaker meetings and Quaker ways. In fact, he had sent his son Tom to the Quaker preparatory school at Penketh as early as 1862.

Marsden Friends Meeting House

In July 1867, Samuel P wrote to William Ecroyd of Marsden Friends Meeting:

                Gasworks Burnley.
                29th 7th mo. 1867.

Esteemed Friend,
    Wm. Ecroyd.

I have felt for some time past a growing conviction that it is my duty to unite myself more closely with the Society of Friends, though it cannot increase my love and desire to wait upon God along with his people. Yet after carefully considering the subject, seeking that guidance of the Holy Spirit, I think the time has arrived when I should make application for admission that I may both by precept and example be better enabled to train and educate my children in accordance with the principles of the Society.

I shall feel obliged if thou wilt bring forward my application.

    I am thy Friend,
        Samuel Petty Leather.

The reply came a few weeks later after going before the 'Committee':

                Lomeshaye,
                Burnley.
                7. 9mo. 1867.

Dear Friend,
    Saml P Leather.

I was requested by the Monthly Meeting to inform thee that thy request to be admitted into membership with the Society of Friends is complied with. The expression of Friends on the report of the Committee being read, was cordial and unanimous. I need not assure thee how pleasing it is to me and others of our little meeting that this is so, and I trust it will be strengthening to

thyself and thy dear wife and children, to be all united in fellowship with the same Christian society.
  I am with love, thy friend sincerely,
    Wm. Ecroyd.

This was a significant step for Samuel P, not only for himself but for his descendants, most of whom are still connected to, or influenced by, The Society of Friends. The Annual Monitor describes his association with Marsden meeting as follows:-
'...he became a diligent attender at the meeting at Marsden, and though this involved a walk of several miles, he allowed neither heat nor storm to prevent his regular attendance. He was there received as a member of the Society of Friends, and became one of its most loyal and generous supporters, and held the offices of Overseer and Elder to the comfort and satisfaction of Friends.'

LIFE AND HEALTH OF TOM TURNER LEATHER   The photograph shows Tom to have a squint though he probably enjoyed normal health until 1867 or early 1868 — or 18 months to two years before he died. In a letter from home, his father says he is going over to see him 'when I hope to find thee in good health and improving' and, 'I could do with thee to assist me now if it could be.' Tom was almost fourteen years old then, at Plumgarths in Kendal.
  Six months later, John, aged eight, wrote the following letter to Tom which contains an amusing family mix-up when John was travelling from Liverpool to Burnley by train.

                                    Gasworks Burnley.
                                    June 25th 1868.
My dear Brother,
            I am very sorry that you are worse but I hope by the aid of your heavenly Father that you will soon

improve. I started at Liverpool and went to Preston and Papa said he would meet me at Accrington. As I was looking out at Preston I saw Mama. She told me to get out and I got out and waited half an hour and then I got into an express to Burnley without stopping and Papa instead of going to Accrington, went to Rose Grove, expecting to meet me, but the express went past without stopping and Papa came back after we got home.

    From your
        loving Brother
            J.P.Leather.

Tom age about thirteen

By August 1868, Tom's health had seriously deteriorated, as the following letter reveals. The letter was written by Samuel P probably to Mary Ann (née Turner) who was then married to Joseph Shaw and lived at Western Bank, Sheffield. Mary Ann Shaw was Samuel P's sister-in-law. She was the oldest of the

Turner family and the two families seemed to keep in close touch. Alternatively, the letter could have been written to Olivia (Turner) Raybould. It is in Samuel P's handwriting though does not have an ending or signature.

The letter dwells almost exclusively on the state of health of the now fourteen-year-old Tom who died of tuberculosis just fourteen months later. Plumgarths may have been a sanatorium in Kendal. Tom's brother John was eight years old then. There are many crossings out in the letter and this was a rough copy which Samuel P retained. What a miserable time Tom and his family must have had in the last year or two before Tom died. They saw him visibly fade away with nothing they could do to reverse the situation, though they went to endless trouble to see that the boy was comfortable. Samuel P had purchased a wheel chair for Tom's use, and friends and neighbours took turns to stay up with him in his last weeks.

Gasworks Burnley.
19th 8th month, 1868.
My dear Sister,
    You will think it long before you get an answer to your kind letter but I have been so very busy all summer that I do not seem to have had any time for writing. I was glad to hear that you were a little better and hope by this you will have recovered your usual health and I hope you will derive benefit from Harrogate. Poor Tom he is still at Plumgarths and so far as we are able to judge we think he is stronger and more healthy, but the curvature of the spine although altered in form is not I fear much better but we hope that if he gains strength he will ultimately so far recover that any deformity arising therefrom will not be observed, we can not by any amount of words convey to your mind an impression of his state, poor boy. He is so weak in the spinal column that he can not stand properly erect without some support from his arms, he can not dress himself nor even

wash himself properly though the water was placed before him as he sits in his chair. One thing which gives us great pleasure, however, under these very trying circumstances is that the dear Boy seems to put his entire reliance upon a greater power than man. He is of a sweet disposition in a general way but it is more shown now than ever it was.

I now may turn to John. He is in excellent health and, I am glad to say, a fine boy, he is getting on well with his learning, got a certificate at the examination last year and we wish and hope he may prove as good a boy as Tom. Previous to John going back to school we took him over to Kendal to see Tom and it was really pleasing to see the affectionate regard which they showed towards each other throughout the time. Tom appears to have a great influence over John and he talked and read to him and seemed not so much to curb him but to aid and direct him the little time they were together. We went on the Saturday and returned on the Monday...

The last and saddest news of Tom is taken from his own notebook. The little notebook, only three by two inches, black leather bound and lined in gold, was used as a diary by Tom Turner Leather during part of September and October 1869. The writing is in pencil and now rather faint, but still legible. He must have written it with great determination knowing, even at the age of fifteen, that his time was limited.

> Sep 15 1869. I rose about 8 o'clock, sat up a little after dinner, had a pleasant day considering.
> Sep 16 Lord help me and guide me through the day. Had a restless night, bad enough and got up before 8 o'clock. Also a restless day.
> Sep 17 Passed a very restless night. Lord help me and give me strength through the day.
> Sep 18 Just a little better night. Thank God for it and may I have a pleasant day.

Sep 19 Had an average night and a middling day.
Sep 20 Rose about 8. Spent a nice day and thank God for it.
Sep 21 Rose about the usual time. O Lord guide me through this day. Had an average night this last night. Had a rather better day than usual.
Sep 22 Spent much the same sort of day as yesterday. Elizabeth Ecroyd came to see me and brought me a large bunch of grapes. Thank God for all his kindness to me.
Sep 23 Rose about the usual time. Had a nice night.
Sep 24 Spent an average day. Thank God for it.
Sep 25 Had a restless night. Rose about the usual time. O Lord help me on through this day. Help me to bear all thou puttest on me for Jesus Christ's sake, Amen.
Sep 26 Had a middling night. Mary and Thomas Brooks stayed up with me to relieve Papa and Mamma. Had an average day. Dr. Coultate with me in the evening and then John Higgins and Margaret Whittam.
Sep 28 Rose the usual time and spent a nice day.
Sep 29 Rose about the usual time. The Lord help me through the rest of the day. Had a very good night.
Sep 30 The last day in this month. O Lord help me to spend the next month better. Had only a middling day today.
Oct 1 Spent much the same sort of day as yesterday. Agreed to make a present to papa of some links for wrist bands.
Oct 2 Had an average night.
Oct 4 to 8 Nothing passed particular. Have not been too well during this time.
Oct 9 Had an average night. I thank God for it.
Oct 10 the very hot sultry weather made me very dull and poorly at times, great difficulty in breathing but the weather changed a little yesterday and I have been better and I hope if it be God's will I shall remain so.
Oct 15 ...

The little diary ends on October 15th 1869, without an entry for that day. Presumably Tom was too weak to continue to write any more. Dr Coultate, Mary and Thomas Brooks and Margaret Whittam were all close friends of the family.

Two weeks later, on the 31st October 1869, Tom Turner Leather died at Coke Street Burnley. The death certificate gives the cause of death as 'strumous disease of ankle and other bones, one year, certified.' The family have always given tuberculosis (or consumption) as the cause. The place of death on the certificate is: 'Coke Street, Habergham Eaves'. Tom was buried on the 3rd November 1869, at the Friends Meeting House Marsden. The gravestone can be seen there today alongside those of Tom's parents. So Tom died at the family home at the gasworks. This must have been the only place where he could receive all the loving care he needed in his sad condition. Habergham Eaves is a district of central Burnley.

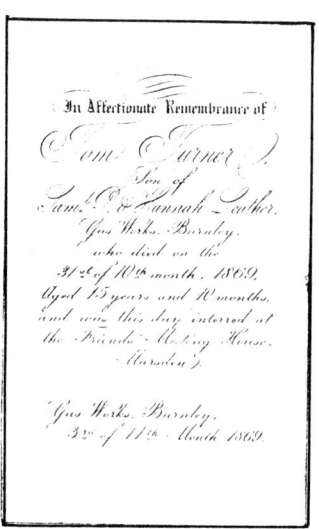

Tom's death was the third great tragedy in the life of Samuel P who had seen his mother go when he was only four, his first wife taken as he was progressing well in his career in Manchester and now, his eldest son, for whom he had had great hopes, was snatched away from him. Life could be cruel, as Samuel P was well aware, and now all he had to live for were his son John and his wife Hannah. No wonder he showed such anxiety and love for John about which he wrote in later years.

Memorial Card for Tom's Funeral

AN EXPLOSION AT THE WORKS   This happened in 1868. There was an escape of gas into a building where a small light was burning, ideal explosive conditions. The result was a huge explosion and a fire. The nearby gas holder was in a bad state of repair and leaks had been daubed with nothing more substantial than grease. The heat from the explosion and resulting fire melted the grease and soon there were formidable geysers of flame spouting from various places in the gas holder, lighting up the night sky. Hundreds of people in the town saw the fires and imagined that the flames would shoot back along the gas mains and pipes to their homes setting the town on fire. People began to panic and move out towards Pendle Hill and wherever else they could escape the 'deadly threat'. While all this was going on the eight-year-old John P Leather slept soundly at his home and missed all the excitement.

HANNAH GOES TO A FUNERAL   In October 1870, Hannah travelled to Leeds to attend the funeral of Elizabeth Glazebrook who died at the age of sixty-six and was buried at Woodhouse Cemetery Leeds. Hannah's mother was Harriet Glazebrook (there are different spellings) so Elizabeth must have been a cousin or a young aunt. Harriet met quite a few members of her family all gathered for the funeral. The letter mentions various relatives and a memorial card gives the details.

> In Memory of Elizabeth Glazebrook who died October 14th, 1870, aged 66 years, and was interred at Woodhouse Cemetery on the 17th instant.

My dear Husband,
    I arrived all safe in Leeds ten minutes past three, we had to wait more than an hour at Halifax, we was told it was on

account of the delays at Burnley I found but poorly not expecting me; they had had William and Olivia over a fortnight since and they promised them they would let us know. Aunt Bessy had expressed many[?] times since they was here, how it was I did not come. Elizabeth and Nicholson was down last night and I am expecting him down for me this morning to take me up to dinner, it is very wet here.

There is a letter come from Sister Shaw saying she can not be able to come as she has had her daughter ill in a fever and is only able at present to sit up a little in the middle of the day. There has been no answer from Rotherham yet. There are some from York expected tomorrow, the day they inter. I have to go out to sleep. I shall write again and when I shall be at home so with my very dear love, I remain thy affectionate wife,
    Hannah Leather.
                      Aunt sends her love.

William and Olivia, Hannah's sister and brother-in-law, were Mr and Mrs Raybould from Greasbrough near Rotherham. Aunt Bessy may be the person whose funeral it is. Sister Shaw is Mary Ann, Hannah's oldest sister and wife of Joseph Shaw of Sheffield. It would be interesting to know who might have arrived from Rotherham or York. Elizabeth Glazebrook lived in Leeds with her sister Ann who wrote to Hannah a year later.

SAMUEL P'S SALARY   Towards the end of 1870, Samuel P made informal enquiries about a pay rise. He was on £200 a year. Then in April 1871, he was invited to apply for the post of Gas Manager in Rochdale, where the salary was to be around £300. But he would stay in Burnley for less than he could get in Rochdale, considering that he was settled there and would have the trouble of moving house. So further representations were made to the Town Council for a pay increase of £50, to make it £250. A report of the council meeting appeared in the local press:

A BURNLEY DIARY   Wednesday, 3rd May 1871. All very ordinary at the meeting of the Town Council except that Mr Leather applied for another £50 a year, making £250 in all, and as he put it in Dr Coultate's hands (being also a Liberal and Chairman of the Gas Committee) the matter went through very smoothly indeed without opposition. Dr Coultate had made enquiries as to how much they paid Gas Managers at a number of towns the size of Burnley. At Manchester, they paid £600. Blackburn, Preston and Bolton all paid £500, but these were all larger towns. Places strictly comparable were Bury, Dewsbury and Ashton which paid £300. Stafford, a smaller place than Burnley, paid £250... To lose a remarkable good man as Mr Leather for a mere £50 a year?...

Said Dr Dean, there are few Gas Managers as good as Mr Leather. Then Mr Wilkinson spoke telling them how clever and reliable Mr Leather was, so that since he came they had not needed to spend a single penny on plans and estimates by specially skilled Consulting Engineers... He had no doubt that by putting in a young and unskilled man in Mr Leather's place they could lose £100 a week very easily, for he doubted if there was another man in the north of England who was such an excellent combination as Gas Manager and skilled Engineer as Mr Leather. In fact it would be a very sad thing for the town if Mr Leather was allowed to go elsewhere for the sake of less than £1 a week, &c., &c., &c.

And in the end, being convinced that Mr Leather is indeed a most excellent and valuable paragon, they agreed unanimously to pay him £250 a year as against £200, on the understanding that he will not seek another increase for several years.

Some years later Samuel P listed his salaries over a period of twenty-three years, from 1864 to 1867.

Figures abstracted from the accounts on 22nd April 1887:
1864: £135   1869: £200   1874: £250   1879: £353   1884: £400
1865: £150   1870: £200   1875: £287   1880: £400   1885: £400
1866: £150   1871: £200   1876: £300   1881: £400   1886: £400
1867: £200   1872: £250   1877: £300   1882: £400   1887: £400
1868: £200   1873: £250   1878: £300   1883: £400

LETTER FROM COUSIN JOHN WILLIAM PETTY IN LEEDS

A letter from Leeds harks back thirty or forty years to times gone by and makes interesting reading. Only a year older than Samuel P, John William Petty was the son of John Petty (senior), brother of Mary Ann Petty and the friend of his boyhood. John William Petty's note paper shows that in 1873 he was a printer, stationer and lithographer at Trinity Street in Leeds. He was in fact a very successful man and the founder, in 1865, of the large printing firm, Pettys of Leeds (now BPCC Magazines) who specialised in printing atlases. The corner of the letter is burnt but most of it is readable including the last page where a few lines are written crossways on top of the writing underneath.

13, Spring Grove Terrace,
Burley Fields, Leeds.
Oct. 18th 1873.
My dear Cousin,
          You will I fear have begun to think me unkind in not acknowledging the very welcome lines you were pleased to send me. When having a few days rest in Wales early last month, I incidentally met with Mr. Hargreaves, and ascertaining that he came from the neighbourhood of Burnley, I enquired if he knew any person of your name — and finding that he did — I gave him one of my business cards, and asked him as he might have opportunity to present it to you with the kind remembrances of him whose name it bore. I was right pleased when I received so early a response to the message by my friend — from my cousin

Samuel. For years past I have frequently thought of you and often longed to either see you or hear from you.

Some three or four years ago I spent a day or two under the hospitable roof of our Uncle Shaw at Sheffield and there heard a little of your whereabouts and success. But apart from that I had failed to ascertain anything of the friend of my childhood — and one who, like myself, was early deprived of a dear parent — and was all but unrecognised by some from whom we might have looked for better things... The lapse of time brings on many changes and yourself and your cousin John William — who more than forty years ago was your youthful correspondent when you were located in Liverpool — have [profi]ted by them.

More than 30 years ago — I married; began the battle and cares of life in the so called land of "us" — and with much comfort and blessing. Three sons and four daughters have been given to us, all of whom, through mercy, have been spared to this day: five of our children have married, two sons and three daughters — and our two youngest children — Benjamin and Sarah Hannah remain with us at home to comfort our declining years. There are in addition nine grandchildren. Dear me! how old it makes one feel, to have to rehearse these matters, and yet cousin, I have only just past my 53rd year. Our middle child — dear Kate — (Mrs. Buckley) you recently saw at Burnley — dear woman — a lively go-a-head... something after, if I have been well-informed, our Aunt Eliza's sort. I can only just call to mind one or two things about my dear Father and Aunt Eliza and have not the faintest recollection of your mother or your father. I dare say Kate would give you some little account of her brothers and sisters, and I need say no more just now.

I hope some day to have a comfortable and long chat with you and then — x x x . Meanwhile I may just add — my years are being crowned with blessing — I have become well established in business which has gradually and safely grown in my hands, and with the blessing of God, I have no fear of wants — I enjoy good health, have been a practical and consistent teetotaller for more than 36 years — am holding on to the ways of Zion — and endeavouring to live for a better world and wish here to do some little good for those around me — and am rejoiced in the thought that most of my children are growing up in the love and practice and the experimental enjoyment of those principles which have been fraught with so much blessing to their dear parents.

Allow me my dear Cousin, to present my kind love to you, to your dear wife and your son, in which my darling wife and all our children join, and believe me to remain,
                    Your affecte Cousin,
                                        Jno W Petty.

JOHN'S EDUCATION On the 7th January 1871, at the age of eleven, John P Leather started at Stramongate School Kendal, run by Henry Thompson. John was there for four years, until he was fifteen. Stramongate School was the oldest of the Quaker schools and boasted the famous scientists John Dalton and Arthur Eddington among its former pupils. The school was situated at the bottom of Stramongate, near the bridge over the River Kent. The school was closed and today the buildings are council offices.

In June 1875, John left school and, for six months, helped his father at the gasworks in Burnley. Then from January to June 1876, he attended classes and studied at Flounders Institute, Ackworth, near Pontefract Yorkshire, under William Scamell Lean with Arthur Eddington, the well-known astronomer, as his tutor. He had board and lodging at the School Inn kept by John and Jane Graham.

In the summer of 1876, John again assisted his father at the gasworks and was, for the first time, put on the wage book of the Gas Department. The three years from 1876 to 1879, he studied at Owens College Manchester, staying at the new Friends' Hall of Residence, Lloyd Street Greenhays, which opened with Theodora Nield as Principal. In the first year John studied for the

London Matriculation which included Latin, Greek and German. He passed with Honours, coming 32nd in the country. In the second year he took the Second Year Engineering course with twenty-four hours a week of practical chemistry. He obtained a prize in analytical chemistry; Williams was the lecturer. In the third year was the Third Year Engineering course and lectures in organic chemistry with Professor Reynolds and Professor Schorlemmer. In the summer of 1879, at the age of only nineteen, John Petty Leather became Assistant Manager to his father at Burnley gasworks.

John P Leather

TWO LETTERS FROM FATHER TO SON The following two letters were written by Samuel P when John was a student in Manchester. He gives news of Hannah who was attending Quaker meetings in Bolton, of his own state of health and of the latest improvements at the gasworks.
Gasworks Burnley.
11th Oct 1876.

My dear John,
         When I cease to feel anxious about thee life will be a burden to me. Perhaps I am a little too anxious, yet I would not have it otherwise. I have no one but thee and all my hopes and

aspirations are for thy welfare and to see thee grow up a good and useful man. I am perhaps needlessly anxious about thee, but I have seen so much evil in my early days and the temptations to which young men are exposed that I could not otherwise and live at ease. Thou must therefore bear with any anxiety; I might have less if I loved thee less.

I was exceedingly glad to hear that everything had gone on well. I am glad thou tried for the Gutrouer Exhibition though thou was so low down. I am glad that thou came out in Latin Higher Junior. I do not think it would have been any worse for thee to have taken the Higher Junior in Mathematics so long as thou could not take the Lower Senior, it would have been going the old ground over again but might probably have grounded thee more thoroughly but of course that is a thing which thou wilt soon see.

I am suffering from a severe cold, my old enemy Bronchitis has taken hold of his old quarters. Mama went last Evening to Bolton to attend the committee on Ministry and Oversight and the monthly meeting today. Margaret and her sister, who is over here, went to Bolton this morning and so here I am all alone. I last night went to hear Mr Hough on Capillary Attraction. He illustrated his remarks with a number of experiments but there was nothing striking.

The machinery has come for the mill which they are now fixing at the top of the scrubbers. It consists of a socket for the top of the centre pipe and a bridge casting bolted to it to carry the step for the shafts. Pressed on the shaft are two plates fixed on it to which is bolted radiating arms to carry the brush wood and then are two bevel wheels. Coldwell says there is sufficient to enable him to finish the interior four scrubbers. We are pressing on with our pipes behind the Engine House all we can. I think I have told thee all now so with love I am thy
       affectionate Father,
        Saml P. Leather

The Burnley Corporation Gas Department
Engineers Office
26 JAN 77
6-o'clock evening
My dear John,
        I have been so busy that I have not had time until now to write thee. I can scarcely answer thy questions correctly and satisfactorily yet we have the Scrubbers on and off once or twice for the purpose of testing the tightness of the Scrubbers, one lasts about 100 cubic feet in 24 hours the other a little more, the water is rather stronger but as to getting the gas free from ammonia I have not accomplished that yet. I fancy that it will take another week to do that for the water in the wells are so impregnated with ammonia that the gas absorbs some from it and then we have not had the whole of the Purifiers changed yet nor the whole of the old gas from the Holders. I hope to give thee a better report next week. The thermometers have been invoiced but have not yet reached here. I will have them fixed as soon as they come. I have a fear that the heat drives the ammonia forward in spite of everything and it will be some time before we get into a way of working the steam jet so as to make them profitable, if we lose nearly all our ammonia from their use we had better return to the old Exhauster. Still it would be well to keep them as a substitute in case of accident. I am thinking of having my old Exhauster put into proper order so that we may of necessity work it and try the difference once more. We get more gas from the Steam Jet Exhauster say 200 cu.ft. per ton that will not compensate for our loss of ammonia by reducing our make of sulphate of ammonia. I must carefully watch this and see what can be done. I shall be better able to say what can be done when I get everything in good working order.

    I sent thee a programme of the Conversazione thou would see, that had arranged to have some of our experiments tried over again, to arrange some of those who would not attend to hear my paper. I suppose there was a very brilliant assembly particularly of the females and that they were so much bent upon the music and dancing that they were impatient both with Mr Faraday and Binyon.

Who is Binyon? It says Curator of the Laboratory at Owens College, get to know who and what he is, and let me know. I heard he is a muff.

I will write thee again shortly. By the way thou wilt be coming home next week end I suppose.

With Mama, T & M Brook and all thy friends love,
>   I am thy loving
>   Father
>   S.P.Leather.

WALKING TOUR OF THE LAKE DISTRICT In the summer of 1877, according to brief notes in JPL's red notebook, Samuel P, Hannah and John went on a walking tour of the Lake District. Hannah was then sixty-three and must have been of a strong constitution to tackle such an expedition. One can imagine her walking through the mountains with long skirts flowing. The party took the stage coach to Grasmere, walked to Wythburn, now partially flooded by the enlarged Thirlmere lake, where they stayed for the weekend. The family continued by walking over the fells to Watendlath and on to Seathwaite in Borrowdale where they stayed with friends of Hannah Dixon, then over Styhead Pass between Sca Fell and Great Gable to Wasdale Head at the head of Wastwater, where they were detained by a storm. They returned home to Burnley from Drigg Station near Ravenglass.

During the 1860s and early 70s Samuel P had purchased and accumulated a large collection of Ordnance Survey maps. As a surveyor himself he obviously appreciated these scientific works of art. He had forty-eight 'one inch' sheets that covered most of the north of England, plus a number of sectioned, mounted and folded one inch maps for use out of doors and thirty 'six inch' maps mostly mounted on cloth and folded, about half of these large scale maps being of the Lake District which was a favourite area. He obviously enjoyed using the maps on his walking tours. He also had a small altimeter in a brass case, fitted in a leather box, which he must have taken with him.

A GENTLEMAN OF SCIENCE   Like many Victorian gentlemen, Samuel P had an interest in natural phenomena and in new developments and advances in science. He owned a spectroscope, an instrument which consists of a telescope and prism mounted on a turntable to measure the refractive index and wavelengths of light from different sources. He also had a magnificent binocular brass microscope with lots of lenses and attachments, along with hundreds of prepared slides in a mahogany cabinet. He was a member of the Microscopy Society and received their journals for several years. Samuel P was also interested in natural history and owned such books as *The Universe* by Pouchet which is subtitled *The infinitely great and the infinitely little* and an ancient and huge copy of Gerrard's *Herbal*, dated 1532. In fact Samuel P had built up a considerable library which on his death amounted to 2,000 books!

Samuel P was a member of the Burnley Literary and Scientific Club, where he read a number of papers both on aspects of gas making and on microscopy. The preliminary meeting to form the club was called by Dr W M Coultate RCS, JP, Dr J C Brumwell, MD, JP and W A Waddington "with a view to the establishment of a 'Burnley Literary and Scientific Club' ".

The meeting took place on the 17th December 1873 with thirty-eight men present including Samuel P who was thus a founder member of the Club. The inaugural address was delivered by the President, Alderman Coultate, on the occasion of a dinner held in the Bull Hotel on the 6th January 1874 and attended by sixty-two persons. Dr Coultate was President for the first five years from

1874 to 1879 and was followed by Dr Brumwell to 1882. Samuel P Leather was on the Committee from 1874 to 1879 and John P Leather became a member from 1878.

Both Samuel P and his son John took an active part in the Club and remained members until about 1885. The Club held regular meetings in the Mechanics Institute with speakers often from outside the town. Subjects of meetings included literature. For example, Charles Dickens junior on his father's works, music, astronomy, archaeology, history of Burnley and its surroundings, geology (speakers included Tiddeman of the Geological Survey and Boyd Dawkins) and other scientific subjects. Topics even included the 'Smoke Problem' and a discussion on the Channel Tunnel in 1883! Between them Samuel P and John P Leather delivered eight or nine papers, lectures or soirées.

S P Leather age 64

Outdoor excursions were also organised by the Club covering many parts of Lancashire and Yorkshire which included those of archaeological, botanical and geological interest. The journals of the Burnley Literary and Scientific Club can be seen in Burnley Library. Here are some of the meetings which were presented by both Samuel P and John P Leather over a period of ten years.

1874 March 24	Paper: "The Microscope" S P Leather.
1874 March 31	Microscope Soirée. Director S P Leather.

1875 September 21st. Paper: "The Chemistry of Coal Gas" (with experiments) S P Leather
1877 January 2nd. Paper:"The Economical Combustion of Gas" by S P Leather.
1880 March 2nd. Scientific Soirée, "Light" by John P Leather.
1881 February 2nd 3rd and 4th. Lecture: "Living Objects under the Microscope" by John P Leather. Specimens illustrating the Structure and Formation of Coal lent by S P Leather.
1881 October 4th. Paper: "The Lower Forms of Animal and Vegetable Life" by John P Leather.
1882 Soirée: A Microscopical Exhibition was held under the Directorship of S P Leather, J P Leather and J.B.Shipley. The exhibits consisted mainly of insects.
1883 February 27th. Microscopic Soirée, "Insects" Directors: H T Ward and J P Leather.

Samuel P was a member of the Institution of Gas Engineers and received the journals over a number of years. Son, John P and grandson, Arnold J Leather followed on and a large collection of the journals, complete up to the 1950s, was eventually donated to Salford Technical College. These same journals were rediscovered by Samuel P's great great grandson, Brian D Leather, in the library of Salford University in 1988, where he was studying electro-acoustical engineering. They still bear the rubber stamp of Samuel P Leather and include papers by John P Leather.

In 1882, Samuel P became an Associate Member of the Institution of Civil Engineers which, on its certificate, states: 'A Society established for promoting the acquisition of that species of knowledge which constitutes the profession of a Civil Engineer, whereby the great sources of power in Nature are converted, adapted, and applied for the use and convenience of Man'. His application was supported among others, by his cousin John Wignall Leather and by I W Wardle, who may also have been a relative. This was a fitting qualification for Samuel P at the peak of his career.

QUAKER MATTERS   Samuel P and Hannah continued to support the Quaker Meeting in Marsden. According to Edwin H Alton's *Story of Marsden Meeting* (1963) 'the Leather family are prominently featured in the minutes'. They regularly attended committee and business meetings, some of which took them to Meeting Houses in nearby towns.

The pony and trap at Marsden

In October 1880, Samuel P purchased a pony and trap from a Roger Preston which made travel easier, particularly up the hill to the Meeting House at Marsden. Unfortunately, on the 14th June 1883, Hannah broke her leg when getting into the trap after a Marsden Monthly Meeting.

THE PRICE OF GAS   According to a newspaper cutting, under Samuel P's management, Burnley gasworks became one of the most prosperous in the country. In 1863, when Samuel P arrived, production was 49,448,000 cubic feet per annum and the price of gas was 3s 6d per 1000 feet, with little or no profit being made. By 1871, profits were so good that surplus cash was used, not only to bring down the price of gas to 3s per 1000 feet, but to help relieve the rates by a sum of £6,666 2s 1d. The price for people outside the borough was still at the higher price of 4s 6d, but, as the borough boundary was extended that year, the income was reduced in 1872 though there was still £2,719 8s 11d transferred to borough funds that year.

Each year after that, the amount transferred increased until in 1879 the price of gas was reduced once again to 2s 6d per 1000 cubic feet. Again in 1885 the price was reduced to 2s 3d per 1000 feet, among the lowest prices in the country. The production of gas by 1888 was 296,096,600 cubic feet an increase of 600% over the twenty-five years since 1863 and, during that twenty-five years, £64,662 10s 4d had been handed over in the relief of rates. Until 1883, gas was mainly used for street lighting and the mellow gaslight of Victorian homes. About that date, however, gas fires and gas cookers were beginning to be used thus increasing the demand for gas. The domestic price today is £3.50 per 1000 cu ft.

JOHN P LEATHER PATENTS HIS INVENTION In 1888, John P Leather patented a new Improved Gas Governor, being a pressure regulator to keep the gas pressure constant whether there is a high or low demand. It was also described as an Automatic Pressure Regulator. Before this time, it was a man's job to regulate the pressure. In 1889, John P sold the patent to R & J Dempster of Manchester for £100, plus a royalty of £1 for every one manufactured.

5. FINALE

For years Samuel P had suffered from bronchitis. For a period of thirty-four years he had lived and worked in or near to the gas works in smoky towns, first in Hyde and then Burnley. In Burnley his house was actually at the entrance to the gasworks. Gasworks in those days created a dirty smoke and fume ridden atmosphere. There were also scores of cotton mills and engineering works in Burnley adding to the smoky environment. Air pollution, together with the damp climate, draughty working conditions, and work often taking place out of doors, inevitably led to lung related diseases. Bronchitis was common and probably started in early adulthood with winter colds which later developed into coughing and expectoration continuing throughout the year. In his later years Samuel P found he became breathless with any exertion as the disease became chronic. Even when he was fifty-five, he tells John, 'my old enemy bronchitis has taken hold of his old quarters'.

He had not been ill in the days before his death but was, in fact, about his ordinary duties until the night before he died. He complained as he went to bed of difficulty in breathing and passed away peacefully in the early hours of Wednesday, the 20th February 1889. He was nearly sixty-eight years old.

His son John later wrote of that night to a friend of his:

I have shrunk very much from writing to anyone about my father's death, although it is but right that you should know a little. His death was so sudden that I have in some ways and at some times hardly realised it even now. He had certainly been much worse for the last two or three months. His difficulty of getting up phlegm had increased and he was easily out of breath with slight exertion, such as walking at all quickly to the post. the last day was one of his better days. At night on going to bed he remarked that he had had a good night the previous night and a very fair day and hoped to get to sleep soon and have a good night. He had of course been about business as usual never having been laid up in the house at all. About midnight he awoke and had a bad attack of coughing or rather of expectoration and got a little relief for a few minutes and then was up again. At one o'clock my mother called me saying that he seemed worse than usual and asked me could I get him some medicine. I did not know that I could. At the same time we were so accustomed for a long time back to his attacks of expectoration that we were not seriously alarmed, only anxious if possible to relieve him. Without entering into every detail, about 20 past he said he would get into bed again (he had been up endeavouring without much success to raise phlegm) and when in bed he breathed very heavily and my mother went out to send a man for the doctor. Just at this time, he seemed to be going to lie back on the pillow, as I held him up in my arms. A moment or two after he quietly ceased to breathe (about half past one).

A copy of the death certificate shows Samuel P to have died at his home at Saunder Bank after three years of chronic bronchitis, certified by his old friend Dr Brumwell, and Samuel P's nephew, James Henry Westerman, who lived a few doors away at 7 Coke Street registered the death. From the obituary in the Burnley Gazette:
'Unobtrusive as he was trustworthy and amiable, MR LEATHER has passed away as quietly as he lived, leaving behind him a most

blameless record, and a memory that will be long held in affectionate regard by everyone who came into personal relationship with him in the busy round of his most industrious and useful life. We may add that MR LEATHER was a sincere Liberal in politics, without any political narrowness, and the last time he appeared on a public occasion was at the Liberal meeting held in the Mechanics' Institution, little more than a week before his sudden removal from our midst. In him the public have lost a faithful servant, his workpeople a kind master, and to the loss his family have sustained we must not presume to refer, except in words of profound sympathy and condolence.'

At a meeting of the workmen at the gasworks on the Friday, the 22nd February the following resolution was passed:

'That this meeting of workmen on the gasworks begs respectfully to tender to Mrs Leather and to Mr John P Leather, its deep and heartfelt sympathy in the great and irreparable loss they have sustained in the death of one who has at all times been a kind, just and generous master, and a friend to all his servants from the highest to the lowest.'

THE FUNERAL The funeral was a grand affair with five carriages and eighty workmen from the gasworks. The workmen hired a steam tramcar from Duke Bar to Brierfield and arrived at Marsden before the carriages. Daniel Pickard led the funeral 'service'. The details of the funeral were printed in the Burnley News:

On Saturday last the remains of the late Mr S P Leather, Manager of the Burnley Corporation Gasworks, were consigned to their last resting place in the graveyard adjoining the Meeting House of the Society of Friends at Marsden, to which community the deceased gentleman belonged. The funeral cortege left the deceased's late residence shortly after twelve, and the hearse was preceded by all the workpeople that could be spared from the Gasworks, some eighty thus attending to pay a last tribute of respect to their former manager. The first and second carriages succeeding the hearse contained the relatives of the deceased. In the first rode Mrs Leather (widow), Mr J P Leather (son), Mrs Raybould, Mrs Fitton, and Mr J H Westerman. The second contained Mr and Mrs Fearnley, Miss Westerman, Mr W and Mr C Westerman.

In the third mourning coach were Mr D Pickard, Mrs Kitching, Miss Greenwood, Mrs Carter, and Mr R Robinson. The fourth contained Alderman J Greenwood JP, Mayor of Burnley, Councillor W Collinge JP, Chairman of the Gas Committee, Mr S A King, Borough Accountant, and Mr E Coates, Chief Clerk at the Town Hall. In the fifth carriage were Mr W Waddington, Market Inspector, Mr S Davis, outdoor Superintendent of the Gasworks, Mr W Williamson, Water Manager, and R S Horrocks, Chief Clerk at the Gasworks. The office staff at the works were represented by Messrs Wm. Pedder, Silas Davis, E J Sutcliffe, R J Littlehales and Wm. Winder.

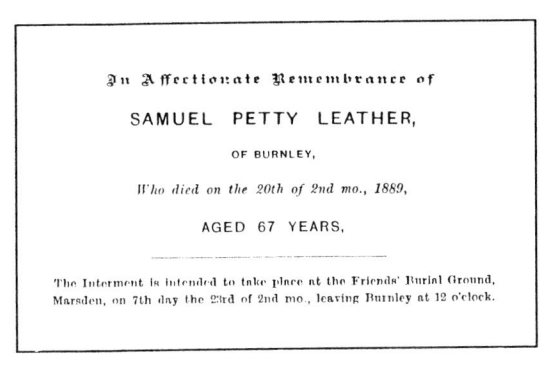

> In Affectionate Remembrance of
>
> SAMUEL PETTY LEATHER,
>
> OF BURNLEY,
>
> *Who died on the 20th of 2nd mo., 1889,*
>
> AGED 67 YEARS,
>
> The Interment is intended to take place at the Friends' Burial Ground, Marsden, on 7th day the 23rd of 2nd mo., leaving Burnley at 12 o'clock.

Funeral Card of Samuel P Leather

At the graveyard six of the oldest workmen under Mr Leather acted as pall bearers, their names being Messrs James Farmer,

Thomas Thornton, James Hopkinson, Robert Charles, Knight Proctor, and John Hargreaves. Mr D Pickard conducted the burial service of the Society of Friends at the chapel and those present having taken a last look at the grave containing the body of their departed relative and friend returned to Burnley.

LAST WILL AND TESTAMENT   The probate of the will was in A J Leather's deed box. It is interesting to note that the will was proved by affirmation by John P and Hannah Leather.

VALUE OF THE ESTATE   John P Leather left a pencilled note of his assessment of the value of his father's estate listing various investments and their value, then itemising every piece of furniture.

Salary due	£32 - 6 - 8
Cash in house	12 - 0 - 0
20 shares in Coffee House Co.	£5 - 0 - 0
10 shares in Craven Bank Co.	160 - 0 - 0
Corporation Mortgage on Security	200 - 0 - 0
10 sh in Bishop House Mill Co	500 - 0 - 0
Loan due from Robinson and Co.	150 - 0 - 0
Cash in Bank	283 - 3 - 2
B......?	88 -14 - 0
Due from Insurance Policy	500 - 0 - 0

He also wrote out the estimated value of furniture and books which gives an accurate account of furnishings and items in each room of the house, building up a visual image of the interior of their Victorian home, including some 2000 books. He does not mention the value of the house which may have been provided with the job, nor does he mention such things as the microscope, spectroscope or drawing instruments.

Drawing Room:		Bedroom (spare):	
Table	£1-0-0	Bedstead, etc	£10-0-0
Side table	1-0-0	Dressing table	2-0-0
2 couches	2-0-0	Wash stand	1-0-0
6 chairs	1-16-0	4 chairs	10-0
1 arm chair	5-0	Night commode	6-0
1 rocking chair	1-10-0	Bed pedestal	10-0
Piano	8-0-0	Wardrobe	1-0-0
Fire irons	10-0	Invalid chair	1-0-0
Curtains	2-10-0	Card table	10-0
Carpet & rug	3-0-0	Chiffonier	10-0
Dining Room:			
Table	5-0-0	Bedroom (JPL's):	
11 chairs	2-15-0	Iron bedstead	4-0-0
Sideboard	2-10-0	3 chairs	7-0
3 bookcases	3-0-0	Carpet	1-0-0
Arm chair	10-0	Bedroom (mother's):	
Rocker	10-0	Bedstead &c.	5-0-0
Sofa	1-0-0	Wardrobe	4-0-0
Couch	10-0	Dressing table	1-10-0
Carpet & rug	3-0-0	Commode	10-0
Fire irons	10-0	3 chairs	6-0
Kitchen dresser	10-0	Carpet	10-0
Hall and stairs:		Servant's bedroom:	
Hat stand & pedestal	5-0	Bedstead &c.	1-0-0
Carpet	1-0-0	Chair & table	5-0
Secretare	1-0-0		
Other items:			
Linen	10-0-0	6 Venetian blinds	2-0-0
Silver	20-0-0	Gas fittings	2-0-0
Crockery	5-0-0	3 toilet sets	200-0-0

Finally, the official value of the estate after various dues had been paid came to £2224-6s-3d. JPL also calculated his mother's yearly income from investments to be £117-3s.

TO CONCLUDE   It is fair to say that his descendants are very proud of Samuel P, of the determination and dedication he had, the progress and achievements he made and the shear hard work this involved. As an apprentice machine maker, waterworks engineer, civil engineer, gas engineer, surveyor, draughtsman, Freemason, works manager, chemist, microscopist, Liberal, Quaker, scientist, family man, and Victorian gentleman with deep religious convictions, he provides us with a fascinating glimpse of times gone by, of trials and tribulations, of personal ambitions, of tragedies and comic situations and of happy occasions with family and friends. He took a great and caring interest in the world about him and in society, being active in many spheres and he made a valuable contribution particularly to his home town of Burnley. People had a high regard for him and he was obviously a friend of many and had many friends. His photograph (on the front cover) shows a genial, gentle, amiable and warm hearted person with that handsome white beard, a hint of a smile and a twinkle in his eyes. He was an inspiration to the many people who knew him and he can still be an inspiration, over a hundred years, later to those who have seen something of his industrious and worthy life.

POST SCRIPT   John P Leather took over immediately from his father as manager of the Burnley gasworks. Two months later John met Mary Swan Reynolds, and by July 1890 they were married. They had three daughters and a son. Two of the daughters, Hannah and Margaret died in their 90s and Hilda is now 99. The son was Arnold John Leather, who became a gas engineer in Blackburn, and who had three sons (John, David and Peter). Samuel P's wife Hannah died in 1902, aged 88, two months after Arnold was born.

GEORGE LEATHER OF WAKEFIELD

Chief Colliery Engineer to William Fenton, Yorkshire 'Coal King'. Engineer of the upper Derwent Navigation, Yorkshire.
Lived Stanley and Lofthouse Gate, Wakefield, then Beeston, Leeds. b. 1748, Woodend Farm, Farnworth Lancashire. d. FEB 1818
= **HANNAH BEAUMONT** ? Daughter of Thomas Beaumont of Wakefield.
bap 10 MAR 1750, All Saints, Wakefield.

POLL(A)Y LEATHER (MARY)

WILLIAM LEATHER
bur 1780

JAMES LEATHER
Colliery proprietor
of Beeston Park Colliery.
b. 21 JAN 1779, Wakefield.
d. 17 OCT 1849, Leeds.
Buried Beeston Parish Church
= MARY TOWLERTON
Eldest dau of John & Mary Towlerton
of Kirkhamgate, Wakefield.
b. 18 FEB 1780, Wakefield.
m. 15 JUN 1803, Wakefield.
d. 10 JUN 1850, Leeds.

JOHN TOWLERTON LEATHER
JAMES LEATHER
GEORGE LEATHER
MARY ANNE LEATHER
ANN ELIZA LEATHER
WILLIAM HENRY LEATHER
CHARLES JAMES LEATHER

HANNAH LEATHER
b 1782
= MILNES

ELIZABETH LEATHER
b 1784
= LONGLEY

SARAH LEATHER
b. 1789
deaf & dumb

GEORGE LEATHER
Civil Engineer, Wellington St. Leeds
Engineer of Aire and Calder Navigation.
b. 5 OCT 1786, Stanley, near Wakefield.
d. 2 APR 1870 (aged 83) (WILL)
= SARAH WIGNALL
Daughter of John Wignall of Keighley.
b. 26 FEB 1787, Keighley, W. Yorkshire.
m. 1809, Wakefield.
d. 28 OCT 1866

JOHN WIGNALL LEATHER
MARIA LEATHER
GEORGE LEATHER
GEORGE HENRY LEATHER
SARAH ANNA LEATHER
WILLIAM BEAUMONT LEATHER
SAMUEL LEATHER
CATHERINE JANE LEATHER
ISABELLA LEATHER

RACHEL LEATHER
b 1790

RUTH LEATHER
b. 1797
= CRAMPTON

JOHN LEATHER
Architect and Surveyor
in Sheffield and Liverpool.
bap 6 MAY 1796, Wakefield.
d. 22 OCT 1867, Liverpool.
= 1 MARY ANN PETTY
Daughter of Samuel and Ann Petty
of Beeston, Leeds.
b. 3 JAN 1799, Beeston, Leeds.
m. 15 MAY 1820, Leeds Parish Ch.
d. 13 MAY 1825, Sheffield
= 2 JANE KENNERLEY
m. about 1830

SAMUEL PETTY LEATHER
MARY ANN LEATHER
EDWARD KENNERLEY LEATHER
ELIZA JANE LEATHER
MARY ANN LEATHER
ALEXANDRINA VICTORIA LEATHER
GEORGE NICHOLSON LEATHER
HANNAH LEATHER

SAMUEL PETTY LEATHER OF BURNLEY

Engineer and Manager, Gasworks, Burnley (1863-1889). b. 8 APR 1821, Sheffield.
d. 20 FEB 1889, Burnley.
1 = **JANE ANN TURNER**
Youngest dau of Noah & Harriet (Glaizebrook) Turner of Rotherham.
b. 27 JUL 1825, Hunslet.
m. 22 SEP 1846, Rotherham Parish Church.
d. 16 JAN 1852, Manchester.
2 = **HANNAH TURNER**
Daughter of Noah & Harriet (Glaizebrook) Turner of Rotherham.
b. 25 JAN 1814, Masborough, Rotherham.
m. 17 FEB 1853, Stockport, Cheshire.
d. 4 DEC 1902, Burnley, Lancashire (age 88).

TOM TURNER LEATHER
b. 31 DEC 1853, Stockport.
d. 31 OCT 1869, Burnley.
(of TB, age 15yr 10mos)

JOHN PETTY LEATHER
Manager Burnley Gas Works (1889-1924).
b. 2 DEC 1859, Hyde, Cheshire.
d. 24 DEC 1929, Letchworth Hosp.
= **MARY SWAN REYNOLDS**
dau of George & Jemima (Dale) Reynolds of Rochester, Kent. b. 26 DEC 1862, Sittingbourne, Kent.
m. 16 JUL 1890, Croydon FMH.
d. 19 DEC 1943, Letchworth.

HILDA MARY LEATHER
b. 1 AUG 1893
= ROGER GIBBINS
b. 30 OCT 1891
m. 26 SEP 1928
d. 4 OCT 1967

MARGARET LEATHER
b. 25 DEC 1894
d. 26 JUN 1988
aged 93

ARNOLD JOHN LEATHER
b. 28 SEP 1902
= 1. MURIEL LITTLE
b. 13 JAN 1903
m 18 SEP 1930
d. 20 AUG 1960
= 2. MARGARET WIGNALL COUNSELL
b. 5 APR 1916
m. 28 OCT 1961

HANNAH LEATHER
b. 15 JAN 1892
d. 27 MAR 1989
AGED 97

Deborah Mary Gibbins
b. 1929
Michael John Gibbins
b. 1932

JOHN BRODRIB LEATHER
b. 1931
ARNOLD DAVID LEATHER
b. 1935
PETER MALCOLM LEATHER
b. 1939

SYLVESTER PETTY OF ILKLEY

or Petyt of Hetton , near Skipton and Langbar, Ilkley, West Yorkshire.
b. c 1670.
bur. 4 MAY 1748, Rylstone, near Skipton.
= MARGARET TOPHAM
b. 8 NOV 1674, dau of John Topham of Hetton near Skipton.
m. 16 APR 1696, Kildwick, near Skipton.
d. 29 SEP 1741, aged 67 (Headstone Ilkley churchyard)

JOHN PETTY
bap 24 FEB 1696/7
Hetton, par. Rylstone.

JOSEPH PETTY
or Petyt, Linen Weaver of Langbar, Ilkley,
bap 11 DEC 1698, Rylstone, W. Yorks.
d. JUN 1756, Kirkgate, Leeds.
= SARAH DOUGHTY
of Ilkley, b. 1707.
m. 26 OCT 1731 by licence, Otley parish church.

SUSANNAH PETTY (Petyt)
bap 17 AUG 1701,
Ilkley parish church.
= EDMUND GARFUTT
of Bell Busk.
m. 9 FEB 1725/6

? HANNAH PETTY
d. 1768

MICAH PETTY
b. 6 JAN 1749, Ilkley.
= 1. MARY STARKIE
m. 1773.
= 2. MARY NELSON
b. 1763, m. 1783, d. 1837.
/\
(10 children)

ABIGAIL PETTY
b. 14 APR 1732, B.Abbey.
= THOMAS LANE,
b. 5 MAR 1732, Bolton Abbey.
m. 24 APR 1753, Bolton Abbey.

DINAH PETTY (of Kirkgate, Leeds)
bap 14 AUG 1743, Ilkley, West Yorks.
(m. Thomas Lindall, 25 DEC 1768, Leeds)

SAMUEL PETTY (baker)   ANN LINDALL
b 21 JUL 1766, Kirkgate, Leeds.
d. 6 AUG 1844 (age 78)
Baker, maltster, flour dealer, Beeston.
Beeston, Leeds.
= ANN   —
b. 1767/68.
d. APR 1835, age 67,
bur Beeston parish churchyard
Leeds, West Yorkshire.

8 children. 3 died in infancy. See next page

WILLIAM PETTY
b. 16 MAR 1765
Kirkgate, Leeds.
d. AUG 1767, age 2
of small pox.

SAMUEL PETTY OF BEESTON

Baker, Maltster, Flour Dealer of Beeston, Leeds.
b. 21 JUL 1766, Kirkgate, Leeds.

Children of Samuel Petty:

WILLIAM PETTY
b. 29 OCT 1786
Beeston.

SAMUEL PETTY
b. 26 MAR 1790.
d. 19 DEC 1859.
Earthenware
Hunslet Hall Pottery.
Moorville Terr.
Beeston. Then Burley Lodge
d. 19 DEC 1859. Bur Beeston Ch.
= MARY ANN BULLMAN

JOHN PETTY
b. 28 NOV 1796,
Beeston.
Baker, Meadow Lane d.
Hunslet (1822).
Then Land Surveyor
d 1826,
age 30.
= ELIZABETH HIRST

MARY ANN PETTY
b. 3 JAN 1799,
Beeston, Leeds.
13 MAY 1825,
Sheffield, age 26.
= JOHN LEATHER
Architect and surveyor
b APR 1796, Wakefield.
m 15 MAY 1820, Leeds parish ch.

ELIZA PETTY
b. 27 SEP 1805.
Beeston, Leeds

Children of Samuel Petty & Mary Ann Bullman:

WILLIAM HENRY PETTY
b. 1812, Beeston, Leeds

EDWARD PETTY
b. 1815, Holbeck, Leeds.

FREDERICK PETTY
b. 1820. d. 1831. Aged 11.

SAMUEL PETTY
b. 1821, Holbeck, Leeds.

EMMA PETTY
b. 1823, Holbeck, Leeds.

ELIZA PETTY

ALFRED WEDGEWOOD PETTY
b. MAR 1824, Holbeck, Leeds.

ANNA MARY PETTY
b. 1828, Holbeck, Leeds.

CAROLINE PETTY
b. 1830, Holbeck, Leeds.

b. 1833, Beeston, Leeds.

Children of John Petty & Elizabeth Hirst:

JOHN WILLIAM PETTY
b. 28 SEP 1820, Greenmount Terr.
Hunslet, Leeds. Founder of Petty
& Sons Printers, Trinity St, Leeds.
d. 4 MAR 1900, Beeston, Leeds.
= SARAH STEPHENSON
dau of John & Mary Stephenson,
farmers of Cottingham, near Hull.
b. 11 FEB 1820.
m. 1 APR 1843, Cottingham Church.
d. June, 1881.

MARY ELIZABETH PETTY
JOHN PETTY
WESLEY PETTY
ANNIE PETTY
CATHERINE PETTY
BENJAMIN PETTY
SARAH HANNAH PETTY

Children of Mary Ann Petty & John Leather:

SAMUEL PETTY LEATHER
b. 8 APR 1821, Sheffield.
d. 20 FEB 1889, Burnley.
= 1. JANE ANN TURNER
b. 27 JUL 1825, Hunslet.
m. 22 SEP 1846, Rotherham.
d. 16 JAN 1852, Manchester.
= 2. HANNAH TURNER
b. 25 JAN 1814, Masborough.
m. 17 FEB 1853, Stockport.
d. 4 DEC 1902, Burnley.

TOM TURNER LEATHER
JOHN PETTY LEATHER

NOAH TURNER OF ROTHERHAM

From Brierly Hill, came to Thorn Hill, Masborough, Rotherham, where he worked in Glass Works. 1825-1834: Shop, 65 Central Market, Leeds. House Hunslet, south Leeds. 1839-53: Rotherham. Portrait in pastels, dated ?1850 with ADL.
b. 1785, Brierley Hill.
bap 6 MAR 1785, Brierley Hill, Staffordshire.
d. 27 APR 1853, Primrose Cottage, Greasbrough Rd., Greasbrough, Rotherham.
= HARRIET GLAIZEBROOK
b. 1786.
m. 14 MAR 1807, Rotherham Parish Church.
d. 29 JAN 1857, Greasbrough, Kimberworth, Rotherham.

Children:

MARY ANN TURNER
b. 12 JAN, bap 17 APR 1808.
d 1879.
= JOSEPH SHAW
b. 1798.
d. 2 AUG 1883.

HANNAH TURNER
b. 25 JAN 1814 Rotherham.
d. 4 DEC 1902
= **SAMUEL PETTY LEATHER**
b. 8 APR 1821
m. 17 FEB 1853 Stockport.
d. 20 FEB 1889. Burnley.

JOHN TURNER
b. 30 MAY bap 18 JUN 1815.
d FEB 1865. at an inn, Nott'ham.
= Sarah

HARRIET TURNER
b. c 1817
= SAMUEL BENNETT

Anna Mary Bennett
b. 1846, Otley

SARAH TURNER
b.1819 R'ham.

OLIVIA TURNER
b. 1821 R'ham.
= WILLIAM RAYBOULD
b. 3 DEC 1820, R'ham.

JANE ANN TURNER
b. 27 JUL 1825.
d 16 JAN 1852 M/C.
= **SAMUEL PETTY LEATHER**
b. 8 APR 1821, Sheffield.
m. 22 SEP 1846, Rotherham.

ELIZABETH TURNER
b.1826?
= THOMAS FAWCETT

NOAH TURNER
b.15 JAN 1828, Leeds.

Grandchildren:

Children of Mary Ann Turner & Joseph Shaw:
- SARAH SHAW = ABRAHAM FARRAR Jr.
- ELIZA SHAW

Children of Hannah Turner & Samuel Petty Leather:
- TOM TURNER LEATHER b. 1853. d. 1869.
- JOHN PETTY LEATHER b. 2 DEC 1859 d.24 DEC 1929 = M.S. REYNOLDS b. 26 DEC 1863 m. 16 JUN 1890 d. 19 DEC 1943.
  See Leather tree

Children of Harriet Turner & Samuel Bennett:
- ARTHUR C. TURNER b. 1843/4 Attercliffe. Nr. Rotherham. lived Swinton, Nr. Rotherham.
- HORATIO JOHN TURNER b. 1845 d. 1862. (age 17)

Children of Olivia Turner & William Raybould:
- FREDERICK WILLIAM RAYBOULD
- ALICE JANE RAYBOULD b.1848/9. = BENJAMIN RHODES
  - William R.
  - Harold R.
  - Olivia R.

MAPS

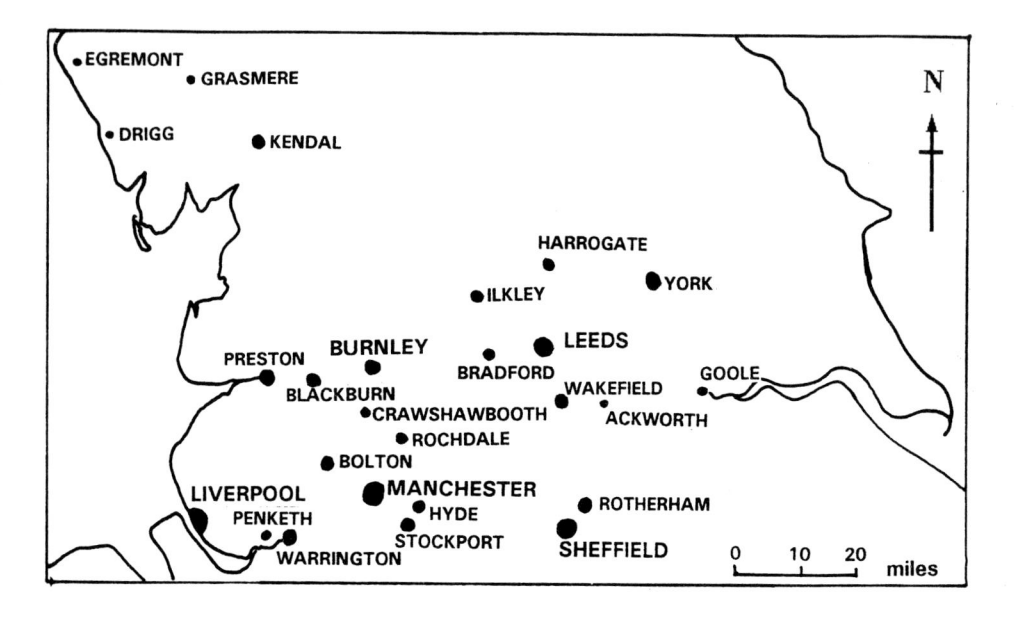

Localities in the North of England

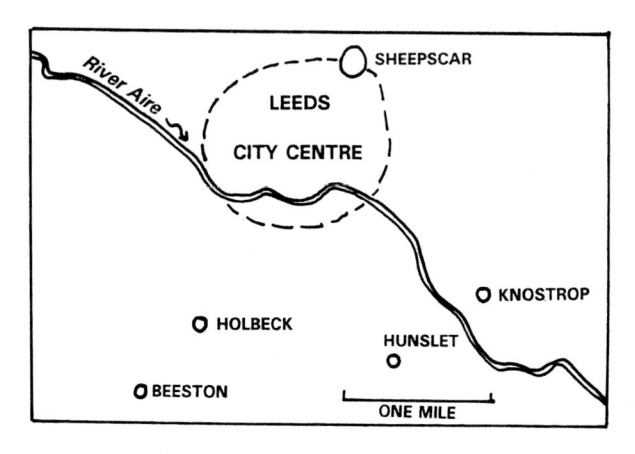

The Leeds area